JEANNE JONES
COOKS FOR LIFE

PHOTOGRAPHY BY
JOYCE OUDKERK POOL

COLE
GROUP

Publisher   Brete C. Harrison
VP and Director of Operations   Linda Hauck
VP of Publishing   Robert G. Manley
VP and Editorial Director   James Connolly
VP Marketing and Business Development   John A. Morris
Senior Editor   Annette Gooch
Editorial Assistants   Lynn Bell, Gina Poncavage, Ann Train
Production Coordinator   Dotti Hydue

Project Coordinator   Raleigh Wilson/Books & Learning Technology
Copy Editor   Ann Weinberg
Design and Production   Vargas & Wilkinson Creative Communications
Food Stylist   Barbara Berry
Assistant Food Stylist   Angelika Muller
Photo Assistants   Jeanette Irwin, Carmen Alvarez, Alejandro Gainza
Prop Stylist   Elisabeth Fall

Text © 1995 Jeanne Jones, Inc.
Photography © 1995 Cole Group, Inc.

Nutritional analysis performed with Micro Cookbook Software, Pinpoint Publishing

Printed and bound in Hong Kong

Published by Cole Group, Inc.
1330 N. Dutton Ave., Ste. 103
Santa Rosa, CA 95401
(800) 959–2717 (707) 526–2682
FAX (707) 526–2687

G	F	E	D	C	B	A
1	0	9	8	7	6	5

Library of Congress Cataloging Number 94-7367

ISBN 1-56426-576-5

Distributed to the book trade by Publishers Group West

Contents

PREFACE

I love food! I love everything about it! I love to eat and I love to cook and entertain—but I also like to look good, feel good, and have lots of energy. The secret to achieving this perfect balance between gastronomy and nutrition is very simple. You can continue to enjoy all of your favorite dishes, so that you never feel deprived or unsatisfied with what you're eating, just by preparing them differently. The goal is to lower the amount of fat used in the preparation of food without appreciably changing the taste, texture, or appearance of the finished dishes.

None of us wants a family member or guest to say, "This isn't bad, considering it's so low in calories and fat." We all want to have rave reviews from our family and friends on our delicious meals and to truly surprise them by telling them after they have eaten how healthy the entire menu was. In this book are 27 complete menus—all of them delicious and low in fat. Several are perfect for parties, and there's even a scrumptious dessert buffet that's delightful when controlled decadence is what you're looking for.

You will also find timesaving tips that include purchasing some of the components for a menu, such as bread or salsa. The take-out departments are the fastest-growing sections in supermarkets across the country, so why not take advantage of them when you're short of time? Although the quality of ingredients is important, you don't have to make everything yourself! Also, many of my menus can be made a day ahead—a great timesaver when you're entertaining and don't have much time to spend in the kitchen on the day of your party.

To help you save time when shopping and preparing meals, I have listed ingredients for stocking a '90s-Style Pantry (see page 147). Notice that I include your refrigerator and freezer as part of your pantry, since you'll want always to have items such as eggs, dairy products, and make-ahead sauces on hand for last-minute meals.

Although there are many ways to save money on food, the best value isn't always the product that is least expensive—especially if the quality of the finished dish is compromised. The integrity of a dish is totally dependent on the quality of the ingredients you use. For example, always buy the most aromatic extra virgin olive oil and the best imported Parmesan and Romano cheeses you can afford (and grate the cheese yourself just before using it). Because the flavor of fine ingredients is superior, you'll generally find that you can use less of them. In the long run, good-quality ingredients don't cost any more and, because you use less of them, they also help reduce calories. Most important, using fine ingredients adds enormously to the taste of a finished dish.

VEGETARIAN MENUS

VEGETARIAN MENUS

Meatless meals are certainly on the rise in this country, with grains and legumes as the mainstays, and with meats, poultry, and fish served more as condiments. Not only are meatless dishes economical, but combining any grain with a legume forms a complete protein. Also, foods from plants are our only source of fiber and contain no cholesterol. These advantages explain the growing popularity of menus featuring pasta, rice, and beans, such as My Favorite Pasta — A Vegetarian Delight (page 3), Chili Carnival (page 7), and Make-Your-Own Risotto Buffet (page 29).

My Favorite Pasta

A Vegetarian Delight

Serves 4

Parsley Salad

Capelli d'Angelo Pomodori Crudi

Fresh Berries or Fruit With Amaretto Sauce

Pinot Grigio or Dry White Wine

Freshness is the keynote of this vegetarian menu: The sauce for the pasta is uncooked. Fresh parsley tips are the main ingredient in the salad. And the Amaretto Sauce is the perfect complement to whatever fresh berries or fruits are in season.

PARSLEY SALAD

DRESSING:

1½ tablespoons red wine vinegar

⅛ teaspoon salt

1 teaspoon sugar

Pinch freshly ground black pepper

⅛ teaspoon dried tarragon, crushed

⅛ teaspoon dried basil, crushed

1 large garlic clove, pressed or minced

1 teaspoon Worcestershire sauce

1 teaspoon Dijon-style mustard

2 teaspoons freshly squeezed lemon juice

¼ cup water

1½ teaspoons extra virgin olive oil

½ cup sun-dried tomatoes, cut into matchsticks

1½ cups parsley, with *all* stems removed, tightly packed

2 ounces imported Parmesan cheese, grated (½ cup)

TIP:

Cutting sun-dried tomatoes into matchsticks is easier with scissors than with a knife.

This is my own favorite salad, but be forewarned: It is so unusual and tasty it may become habit-forming. If this dish has a down side, it's that prepping the parsley takes time. The stems are not used, and there's no shortcut for picking off the tips.

1. Combine vinegar, salt, and sugar in a bowl and stir until salt and sugar are thoroughly dissolved. Add all other dressing ingredients, except for sun-dried tomatoes, and mix thoroughly.

2. Add sun-dried tomatoes and allow to marinate several hours or overnight.

3. Wash parsley thoroughly. Pat dry with paper towels, removing all moisture.

4. Toss parsley and grated cheese with the dressing. Serve on chilled plates.

Each serving contains approximately:
135 calories, 7 g fat, 11 mg cholesterol, 414 mg sodium

CAPELLI D'ANGELO POMODORI CRUDI
(ANGEL HAIR PASTA WITH UNCOOKED TOMATO SAUCE)

MAKES 3 CUPS SAUCE, FOUR ¾-CUP SERVINGS

One of my favorite pastas, this humble dish also is known as Pasta a la Checca. The idea of using an uncooked pasta sauce is said to have originated with Italian street people, who had no way to prepare sauces requiring hours of cooking. Whatever its origins, this sauce is refreshingly simple and good over any kind of pasta, as well as fish or poultry, rice or beans.

2 pounds ripe plum tomatoes (4 cups peeled and diced) (see page 110)

½ teaspoon kosher salt

2 tablespoons extra virgin olive oil

¼ teaspoon freshly ground black pepper

¼ teaspoon crushed red pepper flakes

3 garlic cloves, pressed or minced

½ cup shredded fresh basil leaves

½ cup chopped Italian parsley

12 ounces capelli d'angelo (angel-hair pasta)

1. Sprinkle diced tomatoes with salt and mix well. Place salted tomatoes in a colander and allow to drain thoroughly, at least 2 hours if possible.

2. Combine olive oil, black pepper, red pepper flakes, and garlic and mix well.

3. Add basil, parsley, and drained tomatoes and toss.

4. Cook pasta according to package directions.

5. To serve, place cooked pasta in a large serving dish or, for individual servings, place 1½ cups cooked pasta on each of 4 plates. Top each serving with ¾ cup sauce and garnish with fresh basil or Italian parsley, if desired.

TIP:
Pasta tastes best when cooked only until it reaches the consistency Italians call *al dente*, slightly resistant to the tooth or bite, rather than mushy.

Each serving contains approximately:
420 calories, 9 g fat, no cholesterol, 325 mg sodium

AMARETTO SAUCE

MAKES 1 CUP SAUCE, EIGHT 2-TABLESPOON SERVINGS

1 cup melted vanilla ice milk

1½ teaspoons amaretto liqueur *or*

    1 teaspoon vanilla extract *and*

    ½ teaspoon almond extract

Nobody will guess that you didn't slave over a hot stove to prepare this sauce. Serve it over berries (red or gold raspberries, strawberries, blackberries, or blueberries) or other fresh or frozen fruits.

1. Combine melted ice milk and liqueur or extracts. Mix well.

2. Divide berries among 4 serving bowls and spoon 2 tablespoons sauce over each serving.

TIP:

This easy-to-make sauce is even easier when you use the microwave oven. Simply spoon ice milk into a microwave safe container and microwave for about 30 seconds, or until just melted.

VARIATIONS:

You can make a dozen or more varieties of this dessert sauce by substituting different liquors, liqueurs, and extracts to taste. Try adding a little brandy, rum, Kirsch, Grand Marnier, or coffee- or mint-flavored liqueur. A few drops of chocolate, coconut, lemon, orange, mint, or rum extract add wonderful flavor. I also like to use a little vanilla extract with most of the flavors to smooth out the taste.

Each serving contains approximately:
24 calories, 1 g fat, 1 mg cholesterol, 15 mg sodium

CHILI
CARNIVAL

SERVES 6

Assorted Greens with Signature Dressing
(see page 104)

Quick Chili

White Chili

Red Chili

Black Bean Chili

Colorful Cornbread Balls and Tortillas

Fresh Fruit Kabobs

Beer or Sparkling Water

Chili's rise to stardom on the culi-
nary scene has been due in part
to its enormous versatility. Chili
can play virtually any role on a
menu—appetizer, soup, salad
(served on a bed of greens), or
entrée; chili can be a real
chameleon: red, black, white, or
a variety of shades in between.

QUICK CHILI

MAKES SIX 1-CUP SERVINGS

3 medium onions, finely
chopped (4½ cups)

2 garlic cloves, finely chopped
(2 teaspoons)

1 can (4 oz) chopped green
California chiles

1 tablespoon chili powder

2 teaspoons dried oregano,
crushed

2 teaspoons ground cumin

1 can (14½ oz) ready-cut
tomatoes, drained

4 cans (15–16 oz each) red
kidney beans

Chili couldn't be any quicker than this and still be homemade. Although this and the other chili recipes in this menu are made without meat, you can create new variations by adding a cup of cooked chicken, turkey, beef, or other meats.

1. Cook onions and garlic in a large saucepan, covered, over low heat until soft. Stir occasionally and add a little water or stock, if necessary, to prevent scorching.

2. Add all other ingredients except the beans. Mix thoroughly and bring to a boil over medium heat. Reduce heat to low and simmer for 10 minutes. Add the cooked beans, mix well, and heat thoroughly.

MAKE-AHEAD TIP:
For a double-quick gourmet supper, make this recipe ahead and freeze.

Each serving contains approximately:
280 calories, 2 g fat, no cholesterol, 100 mg sodium

WHITE CHILI

MAKES SIX 1-CUP SERVINGS

One of my signature recipes is White Chili, which won first place for most original recipe in an all-in-fun cooking contest. Later I featured it on a menu designed for a Neiman-Marcus restaurant, where it became one of the most popular items. Try adding cooked cubes of chicken breast, turkey breast, rabbit, veal, or drained water-packed white albacore just before serving.

1. Combine beans, stock, 1½ cups of the onions, garlic, and salt in a large heavy saucepan or pot (see Tip) and bring to a boil. Reduce heat, cover, and simmer for 2 hours or until beans are very tender, adding more stock if needed.

2. When beans are tender, add the remaining 1½ cups onions, chiles, and all seasonings. Mix well and continue to cook, covered, for 30 minutes.

3. To serve, spoon 1 cup chili into individual bowls and top with 2 tablespoons Monterey jack cheese, if desired.

TIP:
Use a heavy saucepan to cook White Chili. In a lightweight pan the liquid boils too quickly, even over low heat. If there is too much liquid left when the chili has finished cooking, stir and let it stand, uncovered, until it cools slightly; much of the liquid will be absorbed. Then reheat it to serve.

MAKE-AHEAD TIP:
This is a wonderful dish for parties because it can be made one or even two days before you serve it.

Each serving (without cheese) contains approximately:
195 calories, negligible fat, no cholesterol, 290 mg sodium

1 pound dried Great Northern beans, picked over, soaked overnight in water to cover, and drained

4 cups defatted chicken stock (see page 88)

2 medium onions, coarsely chopped (3 cups)

3 garlic cloves, finely chopped (1 tablespoon)

1 teaspoon salt

1 can (4 oz) chopped green California chiles

2 teaspoons ground cumin

1½ teaspoons dried oregano, crushed

1 teaspoon ground coriander

¼ teaspoon ground cloves

¼ teaspoon cayenne (or to taste)

3 ounces low-fat Monterey jack cheese, grated (¾ cup) (optional)

TIMESAVER TIP:
Use 4 cans (15–16 oz each) canellini beans in place of the 6 cups cooked white beans. Omit chicken stock and simmer canned beans with remaining ingredients, except for cheese, for 30 minutes.

RED CHILI

1 pound dried red kidney beans, picked over, soaked overnight in water to cover, and drained

3 garlic cloves, unpeeled

2 teaspoons cumin seeds

2 medium onions, finely chopped (3 cups)

1 can (4 oz) chopped green California chiles, undrained

1 tablespoon chili powder

2 teaspoons dried oregano, crushed

1 can (14 oz) ready-cut tomatoes, undrained

Known to have been harvested in South America 5000 years ago, kidney beans can be pink, dark red, or a range of colors in between.

1. Place beans in a large pot and add water to cover by 2 inches. Bring to a boil, reduce heat and cook, covered, until beans are tender, about 1½ hours.

2. Preheat oven to 400° F. While beans are cooking, place garlic in a pie plate and roast until soft, about 10 minutes. Peel garlic and mash with a fork. Set aside.

3. Place cumin seeds in a heavy pot and cook over medium heat until brown and aromatic, about 2 minutes. Add mashed roasted garlic and onions and cook, covered, over low heat until onions are soft and translucent, about 10 minutes. Stir occasionally and add a little water or stock, if necessary, to prevent scorching. Add chiles, chili powder, oregano, and tomatoes. Mix well and simmer for 15 minutes.

4. Drain cooked beans and add them to the tomato mixture. Mix well and cook, covered, for 15 more minutes.

Each serving contains approximately:
135 calories, 1 g fat, no cholesterol, 279 mg sodium

BLACK BEAN CHILI

MAKES SIX 1-CUP SERVINGS

*P*atrick McDonnell, director of recipe development for ConAgra, created this delightful, velvety chili for Healthy Choice® frozen foods.

1. Place beans and the cold water in a heavy pot. Add thyme and bay leaf and bring to a boil. Reduce heat to low and simmer, covered, until the beans are tender, about 1½ hours.

2. While beans are cooking, preheat oven to 400° F. Place garlic in a pie plate and roast until soft, about 10 minutes. Peel garlic and mash with a fork. Set aside.

3. In the same pie plate, combine chili powder, paprika, cumin seeds, coriander, oregano, marjoram, cinnamon, cayenne, and ground bay leaf. Roast the mixture until aromatic and dark brown, about 5 minutes. Set aside.

4. When beans are tender, remove from heat and drain, reserving 1 cup of the cooking liquid. Heat oil in a large pot over high heat. Add onion and green bell pepper and cook, stirring frequently, until soft, about 5 minutes. Add reserved cup of cooking liquid and wine and bring to a simmer. Add roasted garlic and herbs, chiles, and tomatoes. Mix well and cook, covered, over low heat for 10 minutes. Add Tabasco sauce and salt and mix well.

5. To serve, spoon chili into individual bowls and add one or more toppings, if desired.

TOPPINGS (OPTIONAL):
Chopped cilantro, chopped green onions, grated low-fat Monterey jack cheese, whipped low-fat cream cheese, or sour cream.

Each serving (without toppings) contains approximately:
158 calories, 3 g fat, no cholesterol, 318 mg sodium

8 ounces dried black beans, picked over, soaked overnight in water to cover, and drained

6 cups cold water

2 sprigs fresh thyme, or
½ teaspoon dried, crushed

1 bay leaf

3 garlic cloves, unpeeled

1 tablespoon chili powder

1 tablespoon paprika

1 tablespoon cumin seeds

½ teaspoon ground coriander

¼ teaspoon dried oregano, crushed

¼ teaspoon dried marjoram

⅛ teaspoon ground cinnamon

⅛ teaspoon ground cayenne pepper
Pinch of ground bay leaf

1 tablespoon olive oil

2 cups finely chopped onion

2 cups finely chopped green bell pepper

½ cup dry red wine

¼ cup seeded and chopped Texas green chiles

6 plum tomatoes, peeled and diced (see page 110)

½ teaspoon Tabasco sauce

1 teaspoon salt

TIMESAVER TIP:
Use 2 cans (15–16 oz each) black beans in place of the cooked dried black beans. Omit cold water and proceed with Step 2.

COLORFUL CORNBREAD BALLS

MAKES 16 CORNBREAD BALLS

1 cup white cornmeal

1 cup unbleached all-purpose
flour

3 teaspoons baking powder

1 teaspoon salt

4 teaspoons sugar

½ cup nonfat milk

2 large egg whites, lightly beaten

2 teaspoons canola oil

Use this basic recipe for white cornbread. If you want to fill a breadbasket with pastel-colored breads, please see VARIATIONS below.

1. Preheat oven to 400° F. In a mixing bowl, combine cornmeal, flour, baking powder, salt, and sugar; mix well. In another bowl, combine milk, egg whites, and oil; mix well. Add liquid ingredients to dry ingredients and mix just until dry ingredients are moistened.

2. Line a baking sheet with parchment paper or spray with nonstick vegetable coating. Use an oiled ice-cream scoop or a large round soup spoon to scoop out sixteen 2-tablespoon balls, placing each ball on the baking sheet. Bake for 15 minutes.

VARIATIONS:

For green cornbread, add 2 tablespoons of puréed blanched parsley, cilantro, or spinach; for pink, purée 1 tablespoon roasted red peppers or tomato paste with the milk in a blender and add to the dry ingredients; for yellow, substitute yellow cornmeal for the white cornmeal; for blue, substitute blue cornmeal for the white.

Each cornbread ball contains approximately:
79 calories, 2 g fat, negligible cholesterol, 284 mg sodium

FRESH FRUIT KABOBS

MAKES 12 KABOBS, SIX 2-SKEWER SERVINGS

¾ cup each melon cubes, pineapple chunks, banana slices, peach chunks, and whole strawberries

12 wooden skewers

¾ cup nonfat plain yogurt

2 teaspoons honey

This recipe uses a wide variety of fresh fruits. The yogurt-honey dip can be made ahead and stored in a tightly covered container in the refrigerator for up to one week.

1. Thread chunks of fruit onto skewers, alternating colors and types of fruit. Arrange on a serving plate.

2. Mix together yogurt and honey and pour into a small serving bowl. Serve chilled or at room temperature.

Each serving contains approximately:
88 calories, negligible fat, 1 mg cholesterol, 24 mg sodium

CHOCOLATE DELIGHT

A FANTASY BRUNCH

SERVES 6

Chocolate Waffles With Fresh Berry Sauce

*Chocolate Crêpes With
Cinnamon-Apple Filling*

*Champagne, Sparkling Apple Juice,
Coffee, Cocoa*

This nutritious guilt-free brunch
menu is a chocolate-lover's
dream. It contains almost no
cholesterol and is very low in
saturated fat, calories, and sodium. The secret's in the cocoa
powder, which replaces bar
chocolate and the cocoa butter it
contains. Both the crêpes and the
waffles can do double duty as
marvelous desserts.

CHOCOLATE WAFFLES WITH
FRESH BERRY SAUCE

MAKES 6 WAFFLES

1 cup unbleached all-purpose flour

1 cup whole wheat flour

½ cup unsweetened cocoa powder, sifted

½ cup sugar

1 teaspoon ground cinnamon

2 teaspoons baking powder

½ teaspoon salt

1 cup nonfat milk

¼ cup canola or corn oil

1 tablespoon vanilla extract

3 egg whites, beaten until stiff but not dry

This recipe makes six regular-sized waffles, but if you have a waffle iron that makes hearts or other interesting shapes, by all means use it.

1. Combine flours, cocoa powder, sugar, cinnamon, baking powder, and salt and mix well. Set aside.

2. Combine milk, oil, and vanilla; mix well and add to the dry mixture. Again mix well. Fold in beaten egg whites, just until blended.

3. Preheat a waffle iron coated with nonstick vegetable spray. Pour ½ cup waffle batter into the center of the hot iron and bake for about 6 minutes, or until waffle is crisp.

4. Bake remaining batter, keeping waffles warm in a covered dish in a 250° F oven.

Each waffle contains approximately:
348 calories, 11 g fat, 1 mg cholesterol, 415 mg sodium

FRESH BERRY SAUCE:

¾ pound fresh or thawed frozen raspberries, puréed

¾ pound fresh or thawed frozen strawberries

2 tablespoons sugar

FRESH BERRY SAUCE:

1. Strain raspberries to remove seeds, then combine with strawberries and sugar and mix well. This sauce is delicious on toast, pancakes, or waffles. It is also a wonderful topping for ice cream, yogurt, and cereal.

TIMESAVER TIP:

If you're rushed, use a jar of all-fruit preserves instead of making berry sauce.

Each serving (1 tablespoon) contains approximately:
11 calories, no fat, no cholesterol, negligible sodium

CHOCOLATE CRÊPES WITH CINNAMON-APPLE FILLING

The combination of chocolate, cinnamon, apple, and vanilla flavors is a winning one. Be sure to try the Cinnamon-Apple Filling and Vanilla Cream on toast, muffins, or bagels (see page 20).

1. Combine flour and cocoa powder in a bowl. Add sugar and salt and mix well. Add milk, slowly beating with a whisk or an egg beater, then stir in egg whites.

2. Heat a crêpe pan until a drop of water dances on the surface. Coat with nonstick vegetable spray and wipe surface with a paper towel. Spoon 2 tablespoons batter into pan and tilt pan from side to side until batter completely covers surface. Cook until edges curl; flip over and cook other side, about 3 minutes total. Repeat for remaining crêpes.

3. Keep cooked crêpes in a covered container as you make remaining ones. (Place pieces of waxed paper or aluminum foil between them so they won't stick together. Seal tightly with freezer wrap or in a zip-top bag or airtight container.)

4. To assemble crêpes, spoon ¼ cup Cinnamon-Apple Filling along the center of each crêpe. Fold crêpe over filling and place seam side down on a serving dish. Top each crêpe with 1 tablespoon of the Vanilla Cream. You can also serve these crêpes as you would pancakes.

Each crêpe (assembled) contains approximately:
181 calories, 4 g fat, 7 mg cholesterol, 123 mg sodium

½ cup unbleached all-purpose flour
¼ cup unsweetened cocoa powder, sifted
2 tablespoons sugar
¼ teaspoon salt
1 cup nonfat milk
2 egg whites, lightly beaten
Cinnamon-Apple Filling (recipe follows)
Vanilla Cream (see page 20)

CINNAMON-APPLE FILLING:

1. Melt margarine in a large pan. Add brown sugar and cinnamon and mix well. Add apples and cook until they start to soften. Add vanilla and lemon juice, and cook until apples are very soft. The total cooking time should not exceed 10 minutes. Set aside to cool.

Each serving (¼ cup) contains approximately:
103 calories, 2 g fat, no cholesterol, 29 mg sodium

CINNAMON-APPLE FILLING:

2 tablespoons corn oil margarine
½ cup packed dark brown sugar
¼ cup ground cinnamon
4 medium Golden Delicious apples, peeled, cored, and thinly sliced
1 tablespoon vanilla extract
¼ cup freshly squeezed lemon juice

COCOA

2 tablespoons unsweetened
  cocoa powder
2 tablespoons sugar
½ teaspoon ground cinnamon
  Dash freshly ground nutmeg
¼ cup boiling water
1 can (12 oz) evaporated nonfat
  milk
1 teaspoon vanilla extract
½ teaspoon maple extract

This low-fat variation on a popular beverage doesn't skimp on flavor.

1. Combine cocoa powder, sugar, cinnamon, and nutmeg and mix well. Add the boiling water and stir until completely dissolved. Set aside.

2. Pour milk into a blender. Add cocoa mixture and blend until frothy. Pour into the top of a double boiler and heat to desired temperature over boiling water. Add vanilla and maple extracts just before serving.

Each serving contains approximately:
230 calories, 2 g fat, 7 mg cholesterol, 224 mg sodium

BAGELS AND BIALYS

BREAKFAST IN A NEW YORK MINUTE

SERVES 6

Gingerbread Bagels or Bialys

Vanilla Cream

Peanut Butter Cream

Apple Butter

Fantasy in Fruit

Espresso or Cappuccino

This versatile menu is fitting for most any time of the day. It is a wonderful breakfast or brunch and works equally well for an afternoon tea or dessert buffet. By the way, although bialys are usually topped with chopped, sautéed onions, there's no rule that says you can't make sweet bialys as well!

GINGERBREAD BAGELS OR BIALYS

MAKES 12 BAGELS

3 tablespoons decaffeinated instant coffee

½ cup boiling water

1 cup cool water

2 packages active dry yeast (check expiration date before using)

½ cup plus 2 tablespoons sugar, divided use

2 cups whole wheat flour

1 teaspoon salt

2 teaspoons ground ginger

2 teaspoons ground cinnamon

1 teaspoon ground cloves

2 cups unbleached flour, approximately

2 quarts water

1 egg white

1 tablespoon water

Cornmeal, for sprinkling

TIP:

For portion control (and to achieve professional-looking results), use a scale to divide dough into pieces of equal weight.

"**S**imonized donuts"—*that's how Arthur Godfrey is said to have described bagels. Bialys taste just like bagels, but they aren't shiny because they don't simmer in a water bath before baking. This recipe makes a special bagel that you can't buy anywhere.*

1. Dissolve instant coffee in the boiling water. Add the cool water and mix well. Add yeast and 1 tablespoon of the sugar. Let stand until the yeast starts to bubble.

2. While waiting for yeast to bubble, combine whole wheat flour, salt, ginger, cinnamon, cloves, and ½ cup of the sugar and mix well. Add yeast mixture and mix well. Slowly mix in as much of the unbleached flour as is necessary for the dough to become firm enough to lift onto a floured board (dough will reach a point where it no longer accepts more flour being mixed in). Knead on the floured board, adding as much more unbleached flour as needed to make the dough smooth, firm, and elastic. Knead for 10 minutes. (If using a dough hook, knead in machine for 6 minutes, or until of proper consistency.)

3. Place dough ball in an oiled bowl; turn to coat completely with oil. Cover with plastic wrap and a damp towel. Allow to rise until doubled in bulk, about 1 hour. Punch down and turn out onto a floured board. Divide dough into 12 equal pieces about 3 ounces each. Shape each piece into a ball, then flatten it slightly with the palm of your hand. Press your thumbs into the center of the flattened ball to make a hole. Shape evenly with your fingers to form a donut shape. Cover with waxed paper or plastic wrap and allow to rise slightly, about 10 to 15 minutes. (See Variations.)

4. Heat the 2 quarts of water and the remaining 1 tablespoon sugar in a saucepan just until the water is simmering. Carefully place each bagel, one at a time, in the simmering water and simmer for 30 seconds, then turn over and simmer for another 30 seconds. Remove bagels and place on an absorbent towel to drain.

5. Line baking sheet with parchment paper or lightly oil and sprinkle lightly with cornmeal. Place drained bagels on baking sheet. Combine egg white with the 1 tablespoon water and beat lightly. Brush top of each bagel with egg white mixture.

6. Bake in a preheated 450° F oven 20 to 25 minutes or until browned. Halfway through baking time, turn baking sheet to ensure even browning.

VARIATIONS:

To make miniature bagels for hors d'oeuvres, divide dough into ¾-ounce pieces (about 40). Proceed as you would for regular-sized bagels but bake only about 12 to 15 minutes, or until browned.
To make small luncheon bagels, divide dough into 1½-ounce pieces (about 24). Proceed as you would for regular-sized bagels but bake only about 15 to 20 minutes, or until browned.

To make bagel sticks, twists, or braids, roll dough into long strings, about 1 inch in diameter. A single string makes a bagel stick. Twist two strings together for twists. Braid three together for braids. Proceed as you would for regular-sized bagels but bake only about 15 to 20 minutes, or until browned.

To make bialys, omit step 4. Proceed as you would for regular-sized bagels.

Each bagel contains approximately:
140 calories, 1 g fat, no cholesterol, 204 mg sodium

FORMING AND SIMMERING BAGELS

1. Weigh dough and divide into balls of equal weight. Make a hole in each ball of dough by pressing your thumbs through center, then shape into a smooth ring.

2. When shaped bagels have risen slightly, drop, one at a time, into boiling water. After boiling, remove with slotted spoon.

VANILLA CREAM

MAKES 1½ CUPS, TWELVE 2-TABLESPOON SERVINGS

2 cups low-fat ricotta cheese
4 tablespoons sugar
2 teaspoons vanilla extract

Rich and creamy tasting, lusciously low in fat, and deceptively simple.

1. Combine ingredients in a food processor fitted with a metal blade and process until satin smooth.

2. Cover and store in refrigerator.

Each serving contains approximately:
25 calories, 1 g fat, 5 mg cholesterol, 20 mg sodium

PEANUT BUTTER CREAM

MAKES 1½ CUPS, TWELVE 2-TABLESPOON SERVINGS

1¼ cups low-fat ricotta cheese
¼ cup unhomogenized peanut butter
2 teaspoons vanilla extract
½ teaspoon ground cinnamon
1 tablespoon sugar

This unusual blend of flavors stands up well to Gingerbread Bagels.

1. Combine ingredients in a food processor fitted with a metal blade and blend until satin smooth.

Each serving contains approximately:
37 calories, 2 g fat, 4 mg cholesterol, 17 mg sodium

APPLE BUTTER

MAKES 2 CUPS, SIXTEEN 2-TABLESPOON SERVINGS

¼ pound dried unsulfured sliced apples (2 cups)
1 teaspoon ground cinnamon
½ teaspoon ground allspice
⅛ teaspoon ground cloves
2 cups unsweetened apple juice

This old favorite will be just the way you remember it, only better because you've made it yourself.

1. Combine all ingredients in a large saucepan and bring to a boil. Lower heat and simmer, covered, for 20 minutes, stirring occasionally. Remove from heat and cool slightly.

2. Pour into a blender or food processor and blend until smooth. Cool to room temperature, then refrigerate in a tightly covered container. It will keep for months.

Each serving contains approximately:
35 calories, negligible fat, no cholesterol, 5 mg sodium

FANTASY IN FRUIT

MAKES 6 SERVINGS

This beautiful, healthy dessert has become my signature on many menus. It is versatile because you can use a variety of fruits. If using raspberries, you may want to strain the purée for a smoother texture.

1. Place 2 tablespoons of each color purée on each of six large round plates, preferably white. With the back of a spoon, spread the purée over the plate in an interesting pattern.

2. Arrange ¾ cup of the various fruits over the purée, creating a work of art on each plate.

3. Decorate the fruit with the Vanilla Cream.

TIP:
For a professional-looking presentation, fill a pastry bag with Vanilla Cream and pipe squiggles, swirls, and rosettes onto the fruit.

NOTE: Nutritional values will vary depending upon fruits used.

3 cups fresh fruit purée (1½ cups each of two colors of fruit; mango or papaya and raspberry are most colorful)

6 cups assorted seasonal fresh fruit, sliced in different shapes (melon balls, wedges of citrus, slivers of peach, whole grapes, etc.)

1½ cups Vanilla Cream (see page 20)

TIMESAVER TIP:
If you can't find the time to make the Vanilla Cream, serve the fruit with nonfat vanilla yogurt.

ESPRESSO

MAKES FOUR ⅓-CUP SERVINGS

1½ cups water
½ cup finely ground French- or
    Italian-roast coffee
4 lemon peel curls for garnish

This recipe offers classic espresso taste and proves that you don't need a special machine to make espresso at home.

1. In a small kettle, bring the water to a boil. Remove kettle from heat and let rest for 30 seconds.

2. Meanwhile, place a filter in the cone or basket of a drip coffee pot. Place the coffee grounds into the filter and pour ½ cup water over the grounds to wet and settle them. Add the remaining water and let it drip through the pot.

3. To serve, pour the espresso into four demitasse cups and garnish each with a lemon peel curl.

Each serving contains approximately:
1 calorie, no fat, no cholesterol, negligible sodium

CAPPUCCINO

MAKES TWO 1⅓-CUP SERVINGS

1⅓ cup Espresso (see preceding
    recipe)
1⅓ cups low-fat milk
    Ground cinnamon for garnish

You will be pleased to find how easily hot milk froths in the blender, and you won't long nearly so much for a cappuccino machine.

1. If you have a steamer, steam milk. If not, heat milk until just below the boiling point, then pour into a blender and whip for one minute.

2. Gently fill each of two cups with ⅔ cup espresso and ⅔ cup steamed milk, topping with the foam. Sprinkle ground cinnamon over the top of each cup.

Each serving contains approximately:
64 calories, 2 g fat, negligible cholesterol, 99 mg sodium

STUFFED SPUDS

THE ULTIMATE BUFFET

SERVES 6

Vichyssoise in a Spud Bowl

Salsa-Stuffed Spuds

High-Energy Spuds

Twice-Baked Potato and Raisin Pudding

Champagne or Beer

What's the healthiest, most eco-nomical, easiest, most delicious, and satisfying meal or snack you can imagine? Spuds! From soup to dessert, potatoes fit in anywhere, as this all-potato menu demonstrates. Potatoes are an excellent source of vitamins, minerals, and dietary fiber. It's no wonder the potato is this country's favorite vegetable. This menu showcases all the tasty, healthy advantages potatoes offer.

BASIC BAKED POTATOES

Large (12 oz) baking potatoes

This method works especially well for baked potatoes that will be hollowed out, filled, or stuffed, as in the three recipes that follow this one. By the way, the tops cut from the baked potatoes to form potato "bowls" make delicious broiled potato skins. Just lightly brush them with oil and broil until lightly browned and crisp.

1. Preheat oven to 400° F. Wash the potatoes well and dry thoroughly. (If you bake all the potatoes for this menu at the same time, you will need 24 potatoes.) Pierce with the tines of a fork to keep the skins from bursting.

2. Bake for about 1 hour, or until tender. (Allow additional baking time if you bake all the potatoes for this menu at the same time.)

3. Remove potatoes from the oven and allow to cool until comfortable to touch.

TIP:
If you want baked potatoes with firm shells that stand up to being filled or stuffed without tearing, don't rub oil or butter on the skins before baking. Besides adding unwanted fat and calories, the oil or butter softens the potato skins, making them difficult to stuff.

VICHYSSOISE IN A SPUD BOWL

MAKES SIX ⅓-CUP SERVINGS

Serving classic vichyssoise in a potato-skin bowl adds a touch of whimsy to this elegant cold potato soup. Using skim milk and light sour cream keeps the calories and fat content low.

6 large (12 oz) baking potatoes
½ cup chopped onion
¾ cup defatted Chicken Stock (see page 88)
¼ cup nonfat milk
¼ cup light sour cream
¼ teaspoon salt (omit if using salted stock)
⅛ teaspoon freshly ground black pepper
1 teaspoon freshly squeezed lemon juice
Chopped chives, for garnish (optional)

1. Preheat oven to 400° F. Wash potatoes well and dry thoroughly. Pierce with a fork to keep the skins from bursting. Bake 1 hour, then cool briefly on a rack.

2. While potatoes are still warm, cut a thin, lengthwise "top" off each one. Remove pulp, leaving a thick enough lining for a firm "bowl," and being careful not to tear the shells. Dice potato pulp and set aside.

3. Combine potato pulp, chopped onion, and chicken stock in a saucepan and bring to a boil. Reduce heat and simmer, covered, for 10 minutes.

4. Spoon potato mixture into a blender or food processor. Add all remaining ingredients except the chopped chives and potato shells, and blend until smooth. Cover and refrigerate until cold.

5. Pour ⅓ cup soup into each potato "bowl" and garnish with chopped chives.

Each serving (without potato-skin "bowl") contains approximately:
265 calories 2 g fat, 4 mg cholesterol, 120 mg sodium

SALSA-STUFFED SPUDS

6 large (12 oz) baking potatoes

1½ tablespoons canola oil

1 large onion, finely chopped (2 cups)

⅔ cup defatted Chicken Stock (see page 88)

6 ounces reduced-fat sharp Cheddar cheese, shredded (1 cup)

2⅔ cups fresh salsa

¾ teaspoon dried oregano, crushed

¼ teaspoon ground cumin, or to taste

3 tablespoons light sour cream

6 cilantro sprigs, for garnish

TIMESAVER TIP:

Buy ready-made fresh salsa from the dairy case if there's no time to make your own.

This recipe teams up America's favorite vegetable with salsa, which recently beat out catsup as the country's best-selling condiment—a winning combination!

1. Preheat oven to 400° F. Wash potatoes well and dry thoroughly. Pierce with a fork to keep the skins from bursting. Bake 1 hour, then cool briefly on a rack.

2. While potatoes are baking, heat oil in a large, heavy skillet. Add onion and cook over low heat, stirring occasionally, until soft and translucent.

3. While potatoes are still warm, cut a thin, lengthwise "top" off each one. Remove the pulp, leaving enough to form a firm "bowl," and being careful not to tear the shells. Keep shells warm. Place pulp in the skillet with onion, add stock, and mix well. Add ¾ cup of the cheese and again mix well. Cook and stir over low heat until cheese is melted. Remove from heat and fold in 1½ cups of the salsa.

4. Heap the mixture into the warm potato shells. Top each with 2 tablespoons of the remaining salsa and 1 tablespoon of the remaining cheese. Place ½ tablespoon sour cream on top of each and garnish with cilantro sprig, if desired.

MAKE-AHEAD TIP:

These spuds are even good cold and are sure to be a hit in brown-bag lunches.

Each serving (without potato-skin "bowl") contains approximately:
290 calories, 12 g fat, 27 mg cholesterol, 200 mg sodium

HIGH-ENERGY SPUDS

A *wonderful pick-me-up for anyone who wants a quick, delicious way to replenish energy, these low-fat, satisfying spuds make a great breakfast, lunch, or dinner.*

⅓ cup chopped raw almonds

6 large (12 oz) baked potatoes

¾ cup nonfat milk

⅓ cup honey

2 Red Delicious apples, finely chopped

½ cup raisins

1½ teaspoons ground cinnamon

1 tablespoon vanilla extract

1. Toast almonds in pan on center rack of a 350° F oven for 8 to 10 minutes, or until golden brown. Watch them carefully; they burn easily. (Nuts can also be toasted in a toaster oven or dry skillet.) Set aside.

2. While potatoes are still warm, cut a thin, lengthwise "top" off each one. Remove pulp, leaving enough to form a firm "bowl," and being careful not to tear the shells. Place the potato pulp in a mixing bowl, add the milk and honey, and mash thoroughly.

3. Add remaining ingredients, including toasted almonds, and mix well.

4. Heap mixture into potato shells. Serve immediately or refrigerate until cold.

Each serving (without potato-skin "bowl") contains approximately:
437 calories, 3 g fat, 3 mg cholesterol, 258 mg sodium

TWICE-BAKED POTATO AND RAISIN PUDDING

MAKES 6 SERVINGS

6 large (12 oz) baking potatoes
¼ cup nonfat milk
⅓ cup sugar
¼ teaspoon salt
1 tablespoon ground cinnamon
4 teaspoons vanilla extract
½ cup raisins

TIMESAVER TIP:
Baking all the potatoes for this menu at the same time saves both time and energy.

This variation on rice pudding with raisins is one of my favorite desserts. It also makes a fine side dish served with baked ham for an Easter menu.

1. Preheat oven to 350° F. Wash potatoes well and dry thoroughly. Pierce each with a fork to keep the skins from bursting. Bake 1 hour, then cool briefly on a rack. Keep oven on.

2. While potatoes are still warm, cut a thin, lengthwise "top" off each one. Remove pulp, leaving enough to form a firm "bowl," and being careful not to tear the shells. Dice pulp and set aside.

3. Put pulp in a food processor fitted with a metal blade. Add all other ingredients except the raisins and blend until smooth. Transfer mixture to a bowl, add raisins, and mix well. Transfer into a number-7 pastry tube (with a tip large enough for raisins) and pipe the "pudding" into the potato shells. Bake for 20 minutes.

Each serving (without potato-skin "bowl") contains approximately:
130 calories, negligible fat, negligible cholesterol, 108 mg sodium

MAKE-YOUR-OWN RISOTTO BUFFET

SERVES 6

Artichoke Antipasto With Roasted
Red Peppers (see page 68)

Risotto Milanese

Wild Mushroom Risotto

Risotto Primavera
(see Variation on page 31)

Spicy Carrot Risotto

Fresh Fruit

Dry Red or White Wine or
Mineral Water

Perfect risotto demands Arborio
rice, a small, white, opaque
grain from the Po Valley region
of northern Italy, and plenty of
patience. This classic dish requires slow cooking and almost
constant stirring to achieve a
creamy consistency.

RISOTTO MILANESE

3 tablespoons corn oil margarine

1 medium onion, finely chopped
(1½ cups)

1¼ cups Arborio rice

1 cup dry white wine

½ teaspoon saffron threads

6 cups defatted Chicken Stock,
boiling (see page 88)

¾ teaspoon salt (omit if using
salted stock)

½ teaspoon freshly ground black
pepper

8 ounces freshly grated Parmesan
cheese (2 cups)

6 sprigs Italian parsley, for garnish

Saffron contributes to the sensational color and flavor of this Italian classic.

1. Melt margarine in a large, heavy pot over medium heat. Add onion and cook, stirring frequently, until soft and translucent, about 10 minutes. Add rice and stir until each grain is coated and shiny, about 2 minutes. Add wine and cook until almost dry. Dissolve saffron in a little of the boiling stock, then add to rice mixture. Continue to add stock ½ cup at a time, stirring constantly until each addition is almost absorbed.

2. When rice is the consistency of creamy porridge and the grains are soft, in about 20 minutes, remove from heat and add salt, pepper, and 1½ cups of the cheese, reserving ½ cup for garnish. Mix well.

3. Spoon 1 cup risotto onto each of 6 plates or into shallow bowls. Top each serving with some of the reserved grated Parmesan cheese and a sprig of parsley.

TIP:
To make creamy risotto, never allow the rice to become dry. Add liquid as necessary to maintain a "veil" over the rice as it cooks. The exact amount of liquid needed will vary almost every time you make risotto.

Each serving contains approximately:
414 calories, 17 g fat, 27 mg cholesterol, 1173 mg sodium

WILD MUSHROOM RISOTTO

MAKES SIX 1-CUP SERVINGS

I *am delighted to share with you one of my favorite recipes for a truly vegetarian risotto. Rather than relying on chicken or beef stock for flavor, I soak dried mushrooms in hot water and use the resulting flavored liquid in the recipe.*

1. Put dried mushrooms in a large bowl and pour hot water over them. Allow to soak for 30 minutes. Strain through a fine sieve lined with cheesecloth. Reserve soaking water for cooking rice. Wash mushrooms to remove all grit and sand. Remove and discard any stems, and cut mushrooms into thin strips and set aside.

2. Pour strained, reserved liquid into a pan and bring to a simmer.

3. Heat oil in a heavy pot over medium heat. Add rice and stir until each grain of rice is coated and shiny, about 2 minutes. Pour half of the reserved liquid into the rice and cook, stirring constantly until liquid is almost absorbed. Add mushrooms and mix well. Continue to add liquid, ½ cup at a time, until rice is tender and the texture of a creamy cooked porridge, about 20 minutes.

4. Remove from heat and stir in 1 cup of the grated Parmesan cheese so the mixture blends to a creamy consistency. Set aside remaining ½ cup grated Parmesan cheese for garnish. To serve, spoon ¾ cup risotto into bowls or onto plates. Top each serving with some of the reserved grated Parmesan cheese, 1 teaspoon minced parsley, and an Italian parsley sprig.

VARIATION:
Create *Risotto Primavera* by adding a potpourri of lightly steamed fresh garden vegetables. Just stir the vegetables into the finished dish or spoon them over each serving.

Each serving contains approximately:
252 calories, 9 g fat, 11 mg cholesterol, 323 mg sodium

3 cups dried mushrooms (porcini or shiitake)

10 cups hot water

2 tablespoons olive oil

1 cup Arborio rice

6 ounces freshly grated Parmesan cheese (1½ cups)

¼ cup minced Italian parsley, for garnish

6 sprigs Italian parsley, for garnish

SPICY CARROT RISOTTO

2 tablespoons extra virgin olive oil

1 cup finely chopped onion

1 cup Arborio rice

2 garlic cloves, minced or pressed

½ cup dry sherry

2 cups defatted Chicken Stock (see page 88)

2 cups carrot juice

½ teaspoon salt (omit if using salted stock)

½ teaspoon ground cinnamon

½ teaspoon ground cumin

¼ teaspoon ground nutmeg

Dash of cayenne pepper

2 tablespoons corn oil margarine

2 ounces freshly grated Parmesan cheese (½ cup)

Chives for garnish (optional)

Julienned red onion for garnish (optional)

Grated Parmesan cheese for garnish (optional)

VARIATION:

For a vegetarian variation, substitute water or vegetable stock for the chicken stock.

Originally created by chef Matthew Kenney, co-owner of Matthew's in Manhattan, this risotto variation is as enchanting for its spicy flavor as for its vibrant color.

1. Heat olive oil in a heavy pan. Add onion and cook over low heat until soft and translucent, 8 to 10 minutes. Add rice and garlic and cook, stirring constantly, for 2 minutes to coat the rice with oil.

2. Add sherry and cook until rice is almost dry. Add the stock or water and again cook until the rice is almost dry.

3. Lower heat to simmer and begin adding carrot juice, ½ cup at a time, simmering until rice becomes almost dry but always has some liquid covering the top. Add more juice as necessary. Stir frequently. When adding the last ½ cup carrot juice, add salt, cinnamon, cumin, nutmeg, and cayenne. Cook until most of the liquid is absorbed, then stir in margarine.

4. Remove from heat, stir in the ½ cup Parmesan cheese, and serve immediately. Garnish as desired.

Each serving contains approximately:
150 calories, 6 g fat, 3 mg cholesterol, 204 mg sodium

DECADENT DESSERT BUFFET

SERVES 12

Strawberry Mousse With
Raspberry Sauce

Cherry Trifle

Warm Fudge Pie à la Mode

Champagne, Coffee, or Tea

Because everything in this
extravagant-tasting dessert
menu can be made ahead of
time, you can plan to enjoy
yourself and your guests instead
of spending your time in the
kitchen fussing over last-minute
details. And because all the
recipes have been made as light
and healthy as possible, nobody
need feel guilty for indulging in a
little decadence.

STRAWBERRY MOUSSE WITH RASPBERRY SAUCE

MAKES 12 SERVINGS

MOUSSE:

1 12-ounce can evaporated nonfat milk, very cold

2 envelopes unflavored gelatin

¼ cup cool water

¼ cup boiling water

1 16-ounce package frozen unsweetened strawberries, completely thawed

2 tablespoons freshly squeezed lemon juice

3 tablespoons Cointreau (or any orange liqueur)

⅓ cup sugar

SAUCE:

1 12-ounce package frozen raspberries, completely thawed

¼ cup sugar

1 tablespoon freshly squeezed lemon juice

1 tablespoon Cointreau (or any orange liqueur)

Lovely as the focal point of your dessert buffet, this recipe makes an impressive finale for any special-occasion meal.

1. Several hours before you plan to make the mousse, put the can of milk in the refrigerator. Place a large metal or glass bowl and the beaters from an electric mixer in the freezer. (Chilling these items ensures that the milk will whip nicely.)

2. If you will be using a collared soufflé dish, prepare it before starting the mousse. Cut a 24-inch piece of waxed paper and fold it in half lengthwise. Wrap it around a 1-quart (6-inch diameter) soufflé dish to form a 4-inch high collar. Secure the collar in place, using masking tape, and set aside.

3. Soften gelatin in the cool water. Add the boiling water and stir until gelatin is completely dissolved.

4. Place thawed strawberries in a blender. Add dissolved gelatin, lemon juice, and liqueur and purée. Put puréed mixture in refrigerator and take out the milk.

5. Remove bowl and beaters from freezer. Pour cold milk into bowl and beat until soft peaks form. Slowly add sugar and continue beating until firm peaks form. Pour puréed strawberry mixture into whipped milk and, using a rubber spatula, carefully fold together until no streaks of white show. Pour into collared soufflé dish or a mold and refrigerate until firm, at least 4 hours.

6. To make the Raspberry Sauce, combine all sauce ingredients in a blender and purée. Pour through a fine strainer to remove seeds. Cover and refrigerate until ready to serve.

7. To serve, carefully remove waxed paper collar from soufflé dish. Cut the top layer, above the dish, into 6 wedges, placing each on a plate. Cut the remaining mousse into 6 more wedges and place on plates. Drizzle each serving with 2 tablespoons Raspberry Sauce. If using a mold, briefly dip the bottom in hot water, then invert it onto a serving plate. Drizzle sauce over top of unmolded mousse. If you have any leftover mousse, keep it in the refrigerator or freeze it and serve as a frozen dessert.

VARIATION:
Although the strawberries and raspberries lend a lovely color, you can substitute other frozen fruits or fresh seasonal fruits.

Each serving contains approximately:
124 calories, negligible fat, 1 mg cholesterol, 35 mg sodium

CHERRY TRIFLE

MAKES TWELVE ¾-CUP SERVINGS

Anyone who tries this scrumptious dessert will be surprised to learn how triflingly low in calories and cholesterol it is.

1. Combine milk and cornstarch in a saucepan and mix until cornstarch is completely dissolved. Add sugar, egg whites, and oil and mix well. Slowly bring to a boil, over medium-low heat, stirring constantly with a wire whisk until thickened. Remove from heat and add vanilla extract and 3 tablespoons of the sherry. Mix well and allow to cool to room temperature.

2. To assemble trifle, place one third of the cake pieces in bottom of a 2-quart glass bowl or trifle dish. Sprinkle with 1 tablespoon of the sherry, then spoon ⅔ cup custard evenly over cake. Spoon 1⅓ cups of the cherries over the custard. Repeat process two more times. Serve immediately, or cover and refrigerate until cold.

2 cups nonfat milk

2 tablespoons cornstarch

⅓ cup sugar

4 egg whites, lightly beaten

2 teaspoons canola oil

1½ teaspoons vanilla extract

1 eight-ounce angel food cake, cut in 1-inch cubes (4 cups)

6 tablespoons sherry

2 packages (16 oz each) frozen unsweetened pitted dark cherries, thawed (4 cups)

Each serving contains approximately:
153 calories, 1 g fat, 1 mg cholesterol, 96 mg sodium

WARM FUDGE PIE À LA MODE

¼ cup corn oil margarine

¾ cup packed light brown sugar

½ cup nonfat liquid egg substitute

¼ cup buttermilk

¼ cup unbleached all-purpose flour

⅓ cup unsweetened cocoa powder

1½ teaspoons vanilla extract

¼ teaspoon salt

3 cups vanilla ice milk, scooped into 12 balls

Just the name of this luscious dessert is enough to attract the real chocoholic, and the taste will definitely win over everyone else.

1. Preheat oven to 400° F. Spray a 10-inch pie plate with nonstick vegetable spray. Melt margarine over very low heat and stir in brown sugar. Cool slightly, then whisk in all remaining ingredients.

2. Pour batter into prepared pie plate and bake 15 minutes. Lower oven temperature to 350° F and bake 5 minutes more or until set. Cool slightly before cutting. Top each slice with ice milk ball and serve.

MAKE-AHEAD TIP:

Prepare the ice milk balls ahead of time by placing scoops on a cookie sheet, freezing until hard, and storing in a plastic bag in the freezer until needed.

Each serving contains approximately:
163 calories, 7 g fat, negligible cholesterol, 184 mg sodium

DO-IT-
YOURSELF
PIZZA

SERVES 4

Herbed Whole Wheat Pizzas
With Vegetable Toppings

Fresh Fruit With Fruit Purées
and Vanilla Cream

Sparkling Fruit Punch

Invite your guests to create their
very own favorite pizzas right in
your kitchen! Although this
menu's a sure hit with children,
adults also love designing their
own hallmark creations to enjoy
and share with their fellow
"artists." Aprons for everyone
and plenty of hand towels are a
must, and don't be surprised if
you spot some floury faces in the
crowd. By the way, all the recipes
for this menu can be made ahead.

HERBED WHOLE WHEAT PIZZAS WITH VEGETABLE TOPPINGS

MAKES FOUR 10-INCH PIZZAS

HERBED WHOLE WHEAT PIZZA DOUGH:

1 package active dry yeast (check expiration date on package before using)

1½ cups warm water (about 105° F)

2 tablespoons extra virgin olive oil

2 cups whole wheat flour

2 cups unbleached all-purpose flour

1 tablespoon salt

½ teaspoon sugar

1½ teaspoons dried oregano, crushed

½ teaspoon dried thyme, crushed

¼ teaspoon dried rosemary, crushed

PIZZA SAUCE:

1 medium onion, finely chopped (1½ cups)

2 garlic cloves, pressed or minced (2 teaspoons)

¼ cup finely chopped parsley

2 tablespoons water

2 cans (6 oz each) tomato paste (1½ cups)

1 teaspoon dried oregano, crushed

1 teaspoon dried basil, crushed

¼ teaspoon salt

¼ teaspoon freshly ground black pepper

For superior flavor in your cooking, always crush the dried herbs with a mortar and pestle just before adding them to the other ingredients.

1. Combine yeast and warm water in a small bowl and allow to stand for 5 minutes, or until mixture starts to bubble. Add olive oil and mix well.

2. Combine all other ingredients in a large bowl and mix well. Add yeast mixture and stir until dough holds together. Turn dough out onto a floured surface and knead until smooth and elastic, adding a little more flour if necessary to prevent stickiness. Place the kneaded dough ball in a bowl sprayed with nonstick vegetable spray. Turn the ball over to coat the entire outer surface. Cover with plastic wrap and then a damp towel. Place in a warm, draft-free place and allow to stand until doubled in bulk, about 1 hour.

3. Punch dough ball down. You will have 2 pounds of dough, which can be divided into four 8-ounce balls and rolled out to form 10-inch round pizza crusts.

4. For the sauce, in a saucepan combine onion, garlic, parsley, and water and cook, covered, over low heat, until soft, about 20 minutes. Remove from heat and add all other ingredients. Mix well. Set aside and allow to cool to room temperature before spreading over pizzas.

5. Prepare toppings and place each in individual bowls. Set out bowls for guests to help themselves.

6. Preheat oven to 425° F. Spread ½ cup sauce evenly over each pizza crust. Arrange toppings decoratively over sauce. Bake 10 minutes on lowest shelf of oven.

7. Remove pizzas from oven and cover top of each with sliced cheese. Return to oven for 10 to 15 more minutes, or until cheese is melted and starting to brown. Remove from oven and allow to cool for 10 minutes before slicing.

TIMESAVER TIP:
For the dough, combine dry ingredients in a food processor, mix well, then add liquid and blend until dough holds together. Proceed with recipe. For the sauce, substitute a good-quality bottled sauce if you're too rushed to cook your own.

MAKE-AHEAD TIP:
Mix and knead dough ahead of time and refrigerate it up to a day before you plan to use it. Seal dough balls in individual plastic bags.

VARIATION:
You can alter the herbs in the pizza dough to complement the toppings or leave them out for a plain pizza crust.

Each pizza contains approximately:
920 calories, 29 g fat, 66 mg cholesterol, 2217 mg sodium

NOTE: Nutritional values will vary depending on toppings and quantities used.

TOPPINGS:
1 medium onion, thinly sliced (1½ cups)

10 mushrooms, thinly sliced (1 cup)

1 medium green bell pepper, thinly sliced

1 medium red bell pepper, thinly sliced

1 small green zucchini, thinly sliced

1 small yellow zucchini, thinly sliced

1 pound part-skim mozzarella cheese, thinly sliced

FRESH FRUIT WITH FRUIT PURÉES
AND VANILLA CREAM

PURÉES:

1½ pounds frozen red raspberries, thawed, drained, puréed, and strained to remove the seeds

1½ pounds mangoes, papayas, or peaches, peeled, pits or seeds removed, puréed and strained to remove any lumps

3 plastic squeeze bottles, for decorating fruit plates

¾ cup Vanilla Cream (see page 20)

Assorted fruit pieces (use your imagination and whatever fruits are in season): apple wedges (dipped in lemon juice to keep them from discoloring), apricot quarters, blueberries, cantaloupe balls, green or red grapes, kiwi slices, orange sections, peach wedges, pineapple triangles, plum wedges, raspberries, strawberry slices, or watermelon balls

You've never seen true food artistry until you've watched your guests create do-it-yourself designs in fruit. Have several damp sponges and plenty of hand towels handy. Offer paper towels for correcting any minor mistakes or neatening up the plates before the artists serve their creations.

1. Pour ¾ cup raspberry purée and ¾ cup mango purée into separate squeeze bottles.

2. Spoon ¾ cup Vanilla Cream into a third squeeze bottle.

3. Set out 4 serving plates and encourage your guests to use their imaginations as they paint their plates with the red, yellow, and white purées in the squeeze bottles.

4. Then have the guests select whatever shapes and colors of fruits are most appealing and place them on the "painted" plates to create original designs.

Each tablespoon of Fruit Purée contains approximately:
6 calories, negligible fat, negligible cholesterol, negligible sodium

NOTE: Nutritional values will vary depending on fruits and quantities used.

SPARKLING FRUIT PUNCH

Creating a pizza masterpiece is hard, thirsty work, so offer this re-freshing punch to your guests while they are working in the kitchen.

1. Combine all ingredients and mix well. Chill or serve over ice.

Each cup contains approximately:
121 calories, negligible fat, no cholesterol, 8 mg sodium

¾ cup frozen unsweetened orange juice concentrate, undiluted

¾ cup frozen unsweetened pineapple juice concentrate, undiluted

½ cup frozen unsweetened apple juice concentrate, undiluted

6 cups sparkling water

Menus With Seafood

A Romantic Country Italian Picnic

Creole Buffet

Gift-Wrapped Fish – A Present From the Sea

Mexican Fiesta

Help! Company's Coming

Swordfish on Seaweed

The Emergency Gourmet

MENUS WITH SEAFOOD

*Fish has long been known to be the best source
of animal protein because it contains less fat than
either poultry or meat. Fresh fish is also the leading
source of Omega-3 fatty acids, which are believed
to reduce the risk of coronary artery disease. Best
of all, the amazing variety of fish and shellfish now
available in markets all over the country makes
it easy to enjoy dishes such as Creole Gumbo
(page 52), Swordfish on Seaweed (page 73), and
Cioppino (page 77), no matter where you live.*

A ROMANTIC COUNTRY ITALIAN PICNIC

SERVES 2

Tomato and Peppered Cheese With
Balsamic Dressing

Tuscan Bean and Tuna Salad

Herbed Country Bread

Quick Biscotti

Fresh Fruit

Dry Italian White Wine and Espresso
(see page 22)

Here's the ideal picnic menu: You
can prepare it hours in advance
and it still travels well. Pack your
picnic in the morning, head for
work (or a day of sightseeing),
and enjoy a relaxed alfresco dinner at the end of the day.

TOMATO AND PEPPERED CHEESE
WITH BALSAMIC DRESSING

MAKES 2 SERVINGS

½ cup low-fat ricotta cheese

¼ teaspoon freshly ground black pepper

4 slices ripe tomato

1 tablespoon extra virgin olive oil

1 teaspoon balsamic vinegar
  Fresh basil leaves, for garnish

TIP:

Heat affects the character of olive oil, so reserve your best extra virgin oil for uses in which its fine aroma and delicate flavor can be fully appreciated. Use the finest grade for salads and uncooked dishes and for drizzling over cooked food after the cooking period has ended. For frying or sautéing you can use a good-tasting but less expensive grade.

TIP:

Keep the peppered cheese chilled in a small ice chest (which you can also use to chill the wine). But don't chill the fresh tomatoes; they taste better if they are never refrigerated before serving.

One of my favorite appetizers is vine-ripened tomatoes with fresh buffalo mozzarella. In this version low-fat ricotta cheese replaces the mozzarella, so the flavor and texture are similar but the dish is lower in calories, cholesterol, and saturated fat. Freshly ground black pepper adds zest. Balsamic vinegar provides tanginess.

1. Combine ricotta cheese and pepper and mix well. Press half of the cheese mixture into a ¼-cup oiled mold and tap to release from mold. Repeat with remaining cheese mixture.

2. Arrange 2 tomato slices and 1 molded cheese on each plate.

3. Combine olive oil and vinegar and drizzle 2 teaspoons over each serving. Garnish with fresh basil leaves.

Each serving contains approximately:
152 calories, 12 g fat, 19 mg cholesterol, 80 mg sodium

TUSCAN BEAN AND TUNA SALAD

MAKES TWO 1¼-CUP SERVINGS

This salad was inspired by my studies at Lorenza de' Medici's cooking school in Tuscany. There are two secrets to the success of this salad: First, serve it at room temperature, and second, use solid white albacore rather than a softer-textured, darker tuna.

1. Drain beans and put in a saucepan. Cover with water and cook, covered, over low heat for 1½ hours, or until tender. Drain well and mix with olive oil. Set aside.

2. Soak sliced onion in cold water for 30 minutes; drain thoroughly and set aside. Combine lemon juice and salt, and mix until salt is completely dissolved; add pepper and mix well. Add beans, onion, and basil and mix well. Just before serving, add the tuna and mix well. Serve at room temperature.

Each serving contains approximately:
396 calories, 8 g fat, 9 mg cholesterol, 484 mg sodium

½ cup dried white beans, soaked overnight

1 tablespoon extra virgin olive oil

¼ medium onion, thinly sliced

1½ tablespoons freshly squeezed lemon juice

¼ teaspoon salt

¼ teaspoon freshly ground black pepper

2 tablespoons chopped fresh basil

3½-ounce can water-packed white albacore tuna, drained and flaked

TIP:
For the best flavor, add the olive oil to the cooked beans while they are still warm.

TIMESAVER TIP:
When there's no time to soak and cook the dried white beans, substitute a can (15–16 oz) of canellini or garbanzo beans, drained.

HERBED COUNTRY BREAD

MAKES 1 LOAF, 32 WEDGES

⅔ cup cool water

2 teaspoons sugar

⅔ cup nonfat milk

2 envelopes (2 tablespoons) active dry yeast (check expiration date on package before using)

3 egg whites, lightly beaten

1 teaspoon salt

¾ teaspoon dried rosemary, crushed

¼ teaspoon dried thyme, crushed

3 tablespoons extra virgin olive oil

4 cups whole wheat flour
Oat bran

TIMESAVER TIP:

If you can't spare the time to bake your own bread, buy a crusty Italian or French loaf from the bakery.

Besides being my favorite bread (I love the wonderful, rough texture and robust, satisfying flavor), this recipe is quick and easy to make. It requires practically no kneading and no second rising.

1. Bring the water to a boil. Remove from heat, add sugar and milk, and mix well. When mixture is warm to the touch but not hot (too much heat will kill the yeast), add yeast, mix well, and set aside until yeast starts to bubble, about 10 minutes.

2. Combine egg whites, salt, rosemary, thyme, and olive oil. Add yeast mixture and mix well. Add flour, a little at a time, mixing well after each addition. Knead briefly and place the dough ball in a bowl sprayed with nonstick vegetable spray. Turn the ball over to coat the entire outer surface. Cover bowl and keep in a warm place to rise until doubled in bulk, about 1 hour.

3. Preheat oven to 350° F. Punch dough down, knead into a ball, and roll in oat bran. Press the ball of dough into a large, flat circle about 1 inch thick. Sprinkle more oat bran on the baking sheet and place bread dough on the oat bran. Bake 35 minutes, or until lightly browned. Let cool, then cut into wedges and serve.

Each slice contains approximately:
70 calories, 2 g fat, negligible cholesterol, 82 mg sodium

QUICK BISCOTTI

MAKES SIXTEEN 1-SLICE SERVINGS

The name of this cookie (biscotto) means twice-baked. I always try to keep these wonderfully crunchy Italian cookies on hand. Crisper and more flavorful than ladyfingers, they go well with morning coffee, afternoon tea, or fresh fruit for dessert.

1. Preheat oven to 375° F. Combine margarine and sugar and mix until completely blended. Add egg whites and anise extract and mix well.

2. In another bowl, combine flour, baking powder, and salt and mix well. Add to sugar mixture and mix well.

3. Spoon batter into a standard-size loaf pan sprayed with a non-stick vegetable coating. Spread evenly over the bottom of the pan by wetting your fingers and pressing down on the dough. Bake 15 minutes or until a knife inserted in the center comes out clean.

4. Remove from oven and turn onto a cutting surface. Just as soon as loaf is cool enough to handle, cut into sixteen ½-inch slices. Place slices on a baking sheet covered with parchment paper or sprayed with nonstick vegetable coating and bake 5 minutes. Turn slices over and bake 5 more minutes, or until golden brown on both sides.

MAKE-AHEAD TIP:
Biscotti will keep for weeks in an airtight container.

Each serving contains approximately:
47 calories, negligible fat, no cholesterol, 46 mg sodium

1 tablespoon corn oil margarine

¼ cup sugar

2 egg whites, lightly beaten

1 teaspoon anise extract

1 cup unbleached all-purpose flour

½ teaspoon baking powder

⅛ teaspoon salt

TIMESAVER TIP:
Buy your favorite bakery biscotti if there's no time to make your own.

CREOLE BUFFET

SERVES 8

Creole Gumbo

Light 'n' "Dirty" Rice

Cornbread Sticks

Turnip Salad

Turnip Greens With Peppered Vinegar

Crustless Pecan Pie

Iced Tea

This buffet menu features a pair
of Louisiana-style entrées: A light
variation on Creole seafood gumbo
and a low-fat, meatless version
of "dirty rice," the beloved Cajun
dish usually made with poultry
gizzards and livers, ground pork,
and chicken or duck fat. The
tasty accompaniments also are
light counterparts of traditional
Southern favorites.

CREOLE GUMBO

MAKES 16 CUPS, EIGHT 2-CUP SERVINGS

2 cans (28 oz each) ready-cut tomatoes, including the juice

1 large onion, chopped (2 cups)

3 garlic cloves, minced or pressed

1 green bell pepper, diced

¼ cup chopped parsley

3 cups water

2 cans (8 oz each) tomato sauce

½ teaspoon salt

1 teaspoon freshly ground black pepper

2 bay leaves

4 cups okra (1 lb), cut in pieces

¾ pound lump crab meat

¾ pound raw shrimp, peeled and deveined

Dash Tabasco sauce, or to taste

Steamed or boiled rice

The term "gumbo" derived from a West African word meaning okra, or okra-thickened soup. Gumbo is customarily served over plain boiled rice, although in this menu you can break with tradition and eat it with Light 'n' "Dirty" Rice. For the very best gumbo, use the freshest seafood you can find.

1. Pour ¼ cup juice from canned tomatoes into a large pot or soup kettle. Add onions, garlic, green pepper, and parsley and cook until onions are tender and translucent, about 5 minutes. Add canned tomatoes and remaining juice, and simmer 15 minutes.

2. Add water, tomato sauce, and all seasonings, and simmer 30 minutes.

3. Add okra and cook 15 minutes. The creole sauce can be cooled, covered, refrigerated overnight, and reheated before serving.

4. To heated creole sauce add crab and shrimp and cook until shrimp turns from translucent to pink and opaque, about 2 minutes. Add Tabasco to taste. Serve over steamed or boiled white rice.

TIP:
This recipe can easily be multiplied to serve a crowd.

MAKE-AHEAD TIP:
This dish tastes even better if you prepare the creole base (without the seafood) a day or so ahead to allow the flavors to blend. You can also freeze it. Just reheat shortly before adding the crab meat and shrimp.

Each serving contains approximately:
170 calories, 2 g fat, 108 mg cholesterol, 1041 mg sodium

LIGHT 'N' "DIRTY" RICE

MAKES EIGHT ½-CUP SERVINGS

Although this Cajun specialty is usually served as the main dish rather than as an accompaniment to the entrée, it complements the gumbo beautifully. In this lighter, healthier version I have left out the high-cholesterol organ meats, browned the flour for the roux in a very small amount of oil rather than chicken fat, and substituted brown rice for white. The finished product looks every bit as "dirty" as the original.

1. In a heavy skillet heat oil over medium-high heat. Add flour, stirring constantly. Reduce heat to medium and continue stirring until roux is a dark brown, about 3 minutes.

2. Add onion, celery, bell pepper, garlic, and bay leaf, and cook, stirring frequently until onion is translucent, about 5 minutes.

3. Add all seasonings and chicken stock and bring to a boil. Remove and discard the bay leaf.

4. Stir in rice and season to taste with Tabasco sauce. Serve garnished with chopped green onion.

TIMESAVER TIP:
This recipe can be made ahead and reheated shortly before serving.

Each serving contains approximately:
187 calories, 3 g fat, no cholesterol, 370 mg sodium

2 tablespoons canola oil

3 tablespoons flour

1 medium onion, chopped (1½ cups)

1 cup finely chopped celery

1 cup finely chopped bell pepper

3 garlic cloves, pressed or minced

1 bay leaf

1 teaspoon salt

½ teaspoon cayenne pepper

½ teaspoon freshly ground black pepper

1 teaspoon dried oregano, crushed

1 teaspoon dried thyme, crushed

1 cup defatted Chicken Stock (see page 88)

4 cups cooked brown rice
   Tabasco sauce, to taste

4 green onions, chopped, for garnish

TIP:
This dish also makes a wonderful base for using up leftover seafood, poultry, or meat.

CORNBREAD STICKS

MAKES 16 STICKS OR 2-INCH SQUARES

1 cup yellow cornmeal

1 cup unbleached all-purpose flour

1 tablespoon sugar

1 tablespoon baking powder

½ teaspoon salt

2 egg whites, lightly beaten

2 tablespoons corn or canola oil

1 cup nonfat milk

1 cup frozen corn kernels, unthawed

Cornbread sticks are fun for a party, but this recipe works just as well made in an 8-inch pan or cast iron skillet.

1. Preheat oven to 400° F. Combine cornmeal, flour, sugar, baking powder, and salt. Mix well.

2. In another bowl combine egg whites, corn oil, and milk. Mix well.

3. Pour liquid ingredients into dry ingredients and mix only until liquid is absorbed. Do not overmix. Fold in the frozen corn kernels.

4. Divide batter among 16 corn-stick molds or small muffin tins, or pour into an 8-inch square pan or cast-iron skillet. Bake for 17 minutes, or until lightly browned.

Each serving contains approximately:
70 calories, 2 g fat, negligible cholesterol, 183 mg sodium

TURNIP SALAD

Even people who dislike cooked turnips will love this raw salad. Borrow a bit of the peppered vinegar from the turnip greens recipe that follows and try it on this salad as well. If you want an even zippier salad, use a little Tabasco.

4 medium turnips (2 pounds)
¼ cup freshly squeezed lemon juice
1 teaspoon freshly ground black pepper
Lemon zest, for garnish
Lemon curls, for garnish

1. Peel and, either with a food processor or by hand, grate turnips. Add lemon juice and pepper and mix thoroughly. Cover and refrigerate for several hours before serving.

2. To serve, garnish with lemon zest and lemon curls.

TIP:
Sprinkle peeled turnips with lemon juice to keep them white while they are waiting to be grated.

Each serving contains approximately:
28 calories, negligible fat, no cholesterol, 66 mg sodium

TURNIP GREENS WITH PEPPERED VINEGAR

The brilliant green of turnip greens brightens any buffet. Overcooking dulls their hue and makes them bitter, so watch them carefully —they cook very quickly. The peppered vinegar adds zing to these healthful greens.

¼ cup small dried peppers
½ cup cider vinegar
5 bunches turnip greens (4 pounds)

1. Place peppers in a small bottle. Add vinegar and allow to stand for at least 24 hours before using.

2. Dip greens in cold water to loosen any dirt or grit and wash thoroughly. Remove any large, tough veins or discolored leaves.

3. Steam greens until limp and bright green, about 2 minutes. (You can also cook them in a microwave.) Serve with peppered vinegar.

Each serving contains approximately:
17 calories, negligible fat, no cholesterol, 17 mg sodium

CRUSTLESS PECAN PIE

MAKES 8 SERVINGS

1 cup pecan halves (¼ pound)
1 envelope unflavored gelatin
2 tablespoons water
1 can evaporated skim milk
    (1½ cups)
1 cup nonfat milk
¼ cup corn oil margarine
¾ cup packed dark brown sugar
2 teaspoons vanilla extract

A *lower-calorie, low-fat version of a popular Southern dessert.*

1. Preheat oven to 350° F. Coarsely chop pecans, place in pan, and bake 8 to 10 minutes or until browned. (See Tip.) Watch carefully because they burn easily! Set aside.

2. Add the water to gelatin and allow to soften.

3. Combine canned milk, milk, margarine, and sugar in a saucepan and cook over medium heat, stirring constantly with a wire whisk. Just before mixture comes to a boil, remove from heat. Do not boil. (If allowed to boil, mixture will separate and have a grainy appearance. This will not ruin the taste but does detract from the satiny look.)

4. Add vanilla and softened gelatin and mix well. Allow to cool to room temperature and pour into 9- or 10-inch pie plate. Add toasted chopped pecans and mix well (they will rise to the top as the filling sets).

5. Refrigerate for at least 4 hours before serving.

TIP:
If you don't want to turn on the oven just to toast the pecans, you can toast them on top of the stove in a skillet.

Each serving contains approximately:
253 calories, 16 g fat, 10 mg cholesterol, 68 mg sodium

GIFT-WRAPPED FISH

A PRESENT FROM THE SEA

SERVES 4

Chilled Asparagus With Dilled
Lemon-Mustard Sauce

Salmon en Papillote With Couscous and
Fresh Vegetables

Herbed Wine Sauce

Lemon Angel

Chardonnay or Pinot Noir

Baked in parchment paper, this
elegant entrée is easy on the cook
because you can prepare it hours
or even a day in advance for a
gourmet meal served in minutes.
And because the dessert needs to
be made ahead of time, there's no
fussing to put everything together
at the last minute.

CHILLED ASPARAGUS WITH DILLED LEMON-MUSTARD SAUCE

MAKES 4 SERVINGS

SAUCE:

¼ cup fat-free mayonnaise

2 tablespoons sweet brown prepared mustard

2 tablespoons freshly squeezed lemon juice

1 teaspoon grated lemon zest

¼ teaspoon dried dill

¼ teaspoon dried tarragon

2 teaspoons extra virgin olive oil

24 asparagus spears, steamed crisp-tender and chilled

4 sprigs fresh dill, for garnish, (optional)

Edible flowers, for garnish (optional)

This simple-to-make first course also doubles as an hors d'oeuvre with cocktails or sparkling water before dinner. Just serve the asparagus spears separately for dipping into the sauce. I like this sauce so much that I paired it with Romano beans for the Non-Traditional Holiday menu (see page 113).

1. In a small mixing bowl combine all dressing ingredients except oil and mix well. Whisk in olive oil and set aside.

2. Arrange 6 of the steamed, chilled asparagus spears on each of 4 plates. Spoon 2 tablespoons sauce over each serving, garnishing each with a sprig of fresh dill or edible flowers, if desired.

Each serving contains approximately:
68 calories, 3 g fat, no cholesterol, 277 mg sodium

SALMON EN PAPILLOTE WITH COUSCOUS AND FRESH VEGETABLES

MAKES 4 SERVINGS

Cooking in parchment paper (en papillote) is a versatile cooking method that works well with many kinds of fish. For this menu I have chosen salmon for its lovely color. The couscous is quick to prepare; however, you can substitute the same amount of cooked rice. Also, you can vary the herb blend to take advantage of whatever herbs are available at the market or are growing in your garden.

1. Preheat oven to 350° F. To make couscous, combine stock, salt, pepper, olive oil and bay leaf in a saucepan with a tight-fitting lid; bring to a boil. Add couscous and mix well; remove from heat. Cover tightly and allow to stand 5 minutes or until all liquid has been absorbed.

2. Cut parchment paper into large hearts by folding each piece of paper in half and then cutting the folded paper into a half-heart shape. Unfold hearts and spoon ½ cup couscous onto center of one side of each heart. Top each serving with ½ cup zucchini strips, a piece of the salmon fillet, and ¼ cup diced tomato. Sprinkle one fourth of the chopped olives on each serving, and top with ¼ teaspoon of each of the fresh herbs.

3. To seal parchment hearts, brush edges with beaten egg. Fold empty half of each heart carefully over contents, pressing edges together. Fold edges over, starting at top with a small fold and continuing all the way around with overlapping folds. Crimp edges tightly with your fingers.

4. Place packets on baking sheets, two per sheet, and bake 12 minutes. Alternatively, you can assemble the packets in the morning or even the night before. Half an hour before mealtime, remove baking sheets from refrigerator, allow packets to warm to room temperature, and bake 12 minutes.

5. To serve, place each packet on a large plate and cut an X on top of each. Fold back corners of the X and spoon 3 tablespoons heated Herbed Wine Sauce over each helping.

Each serving contains approximately:
485 calories, 17 g fat, 74 mg cholesterol, 183 mg sodium

1½ cups defatted Chicken Stock (see page 88)

½ teaspoon salt (omit if using salted stock)

¼ teaspoon freshly ground black pepper

2 teaspoons extra virgin olive oil

1 bay leaf

1 cup (6⅔ oz) couscous

4 sheets parchment paper (about 20 by 20 inches each)

2 small zucchini (8 oz), cut in matchstick-size strips (2 cups)

1 pound fresh salmon fillet, cut into four 4-ounce pieces

4 plum tomatoes (8 oz), peeled and diced (1 cup)

8 black olives, finely chopped

1 teaspoon each finely chopped fresh basil, thyme, tarragon, parsley, and chives

1 egg, lightly beaten (to seal the edges of the paper)

¾ cup Herbed Wine Sauce (see page 60)

TIP:

You can buy parchment paper for pennies a sheet at most bakeries or in rolls at cooks' supply stores and some supermarkets. And although the parchment makes a much more attractive presentation, you can substitute aluminum foil.

HERBED WINE SAUCE

MAKES ABOUT ¾ CUP SAUCE, FOUR 3-TABLESPOON SERVINGS

1 medium onion, coarsely
   chopped (1½ cups)
2 garlic cloves, quartered
1 tablespoon chopped fresh
   thyme
¼ cup chopped fresh tarragon
½ cup chopped fresh basil
1 cup dry white wine
2 teaspoons extra virgin olive oil

The sauce for the salmon can also be made ahead, stored in the refrigerator, and reheated just before serving.

1. Combine all ingredients except oil in a blender and purée.

1. Pour into a small saucepan and bring to a boil over medium heat. Reduce heat to low and simmer until the sauce is reduced by half.

3. Strain reduced sauce, pressing all liquid through strainer with the back of a spoon. Slowly whisk in olive oil until smooth.

Each serving contains approximately:
51 calories, 3 g fat, no cholesterol, 3 mg sodium

LEMON ANGEL

MAKES 8 SERVINGS

3 tablespoons corn oil margarine
1 cup sugar
¾ cup freshly squeezed lemon
   juice
1 tablespoon grated lemon zest
2 eggs
6 egg whites
   One 8-ounce angel food cake,
   thinly sliced

TIP:
If you have any cake left over, it
freezes beautifully.

This delicious and refreshingly light dessert does have to be made in advance because it needs time to set. The original recipe was given to me by my good friend, Betty DeBakcsy, and it is still my favorite adaptation of a traditionally rich recipe.

1. Combine margarine and sugar in the top of a double boiler. Cook and stir over medium-high heat until well mixed and margarine is melted. Add lemon juice and grated zest and mix well.

2. Combine eggs and egg whites and beat until frothy. Add to sugar mixture and cook, stirring constantly, until thick, about 10 minutes. Remove from heat and allow to cool slightly.

3. Place one third of the cake slices in bottom of a soufflé dish. Cover with 1 cup of the lemon sauce. Repeat layers two more times, ending with a layer of lemon sauce on top. Cover tightly and refrigerate for at least 6 hours or overnight before serving.

Each serving contains approximately:
250 calories, 6 g fat, 53 mg cholesterol, 185 mg sodium

MEXICAN FIESTA

SERVES 6

Asparagus Guacamole

Fat-Free Tortilla Wedges

Confetti Salad

*Soft Prawn Tacos With
Papaya Salsa*

Flan

*Make-Believe Margaritas
and Nonalcoholic Beer*

Mexican food is not only delicious, it's a snap to make and
serve. The guacamole tastes all
the better for having been made
several hours ahead or even the
night before, and the flan can
also be prepared a day in
advance.

ASPARAGUS GUACAMOLE

MAKES TWELVE ¼-CUP SERVINGS

2 cups chopped lightly steamed asparagus

2½ teaspoons freshly squeezed lemon juice

3 tablespoons chopped onion

1 large tomato, chopped (1 cup)

¾ teaspoon salt (optional)

½ teaspoon chili powder

¼ teaspoon ground cumin

¼ teaspoon freshly ground black pepper

1 garlic clove, halved
   Dash Tabasco sauce

⅓ cup light sour cream

This version of guacamole is a fresh take on a popular dish. If possible, make the guacamole several hours ahead or even the night before serving to allow the flavors to meld.

1. Place all ingredients in a blender. Blend until smooth.

2. Transfer to bowl, cover, and refrigerate several hours or overnight before serving.

Each serving contains approximately:
25 calories, 1 g fat, 3 mg cholesterol, 154 mg sodium

FAT-FREE TORTILLA WEDGES

MAKES TWELVE 6-CHIP SERVINGS

12 corn tortillas
   Salt (optional)

TIMESAVER TIP:

If you're short on time, purchase fresh ready-made salsa from the dairy case and buy baked (not fried) chips.

Fortunately, now you can buy fat-free chips in most markets. The advantage of making your own is that they are less expensive and always taste fresher than the store-bought kind. For variety, sprinkle them before baking with ground cumin, or chili, garlic, or onion powder. They taste best when freshly toasted.

1. Preheat oven to 400° F. Cut each tortilla into 6 wedges. Arrange wedges evenly on 2 baking sheets and bake 10 minutes.

2. Remove from oven and turn each piece over, then return to oven until crisp and lightly browned, 3 to 5 minutes more.

3. Remove from oven and let cool to room temperature on baking sheets.

Each serving contains approximately:
50 calories, 1 g fat, no cholesterol, 40 mg sodium

CONFETTI SALAD

MAKES SIX ⅔-CUP SERVINGS

You'll love the combination of flavors and textures in this salad. In fact, the taste makes dicing vegetables worth the effort. Sometimes I add diced cooked chicken and serve the salad as an entrée.

1. Dice all vegetables in ¼-inch cubes and place in a bowl.

2. In another bowl, combine lime juice and salt. Stir until salt is completely dissolved, then add remaining dressing ingredients and mix well. Add dressing to diced vegetables and mix well.

3. Line 6 chilled salad plates with 2 or 3 Belgian endive leaves. Arrange ⅔ cup salad on each plate. Top each serving with 1 teaspoon chopped peanuts.

Each serving contains approximately:
105 calories, 6 g fat, no cholesterol, 130 mg sodium

SALAD:

½ jicama, peeled

½ red bell pepper, seeds and membranes removed

½ yellow bell pepper, seeds and membranes removed

1 zucchini

1 carrot

DRESSING:

¼ cup freshly squeezed lime juice

¼ teaspoon salt

¼ teaspoon cayenne pepper

2 tablespoons peanut oil

2 tablespoons rice vinegar

2 tablespoons honey

2 heads Belgian endive, separated into leaves

2 tablespoons coarsely chopped dry-roasted peanuts

SOFT PRAWN TACOS WITH PAPAYA SALSA

6 whole wheat tortillas

6 large prawns or shrimp (about ¼ lb), peeled, deveined, tails attached (see page 78)

¾ pound small prawns or shrimp, peeled, deveined

¼ cup defatted Chicken Stock (see page 88)

¾ cup grated jalapeño Jack cheese

1½ cups shredded spinach leaves

3 cups Papaya Salsa (see page 65)

This taco recipe was inspired by the lobster tacos on Dean Fearing's menu at The Mansion, in Dallas. I have called for six large prawns for garnish and used the less expensive smaller prawns for the taco filling. The perfect accompaniment for the tacos, as well as for broiled fish and poultry, is the Papaya Salsa. If you can't find ripe papayas, use mangoes, peaches, or melon.

1. Preheat oven to 300° F. Wrap tortillas lightly in aluminum foil and warm in oven for 15 minutes.

2. Set large prawns aside. Clean small prawns, remove tails, and dice. Bring chicken stock to a boil in a sauté pan, add diced prawns, and cook just until they turn from translucent to opaque, about 1 minute. Do not overcook.

3. Remove diced prawns from stock and set aside. Butterfly large prawns by cutting them in half lengthwise up the back (vein side) to within 1 inch of the tail. Bring stock back to a boil and cook butterflied prawns until they turn from translucent to opaque, about 1 minute. Reserve butterflied prawns for garnish.

4. Remove warm tortillas from foil and spoon equal amounts of diced prawns down center of each. Sprinkle 2 tablespoons grated cheese evenly over prawns in each taco. Top with ¼ cup shredded spinach. Roll tortilla into a cylinder and place seam side up on a large, warm plate. Top each taco with 1 butterflied prawn. Spoon ¼ cup salsa along both sides of each taco and serve.

Each serving contains approximately:
256 calories, 6 g fat, 160 mg cholesterol, 524 mg sodium

Papaya Salsa

MAKES SIX ½-CUP SERVINGS

1. Combine all ingredients and mix well. Cover and refrigerate for several hours before serving.

Each serving contains approximately:
49 calories, negligible fat, no cholesterol, 125 mg sodium

2 papayas, peeled and finely diced (3 cups)
1 shallot, minced (1 tablespoon)
1 garlic clove, minced (1 teaspoon)
2 tablespoons lightly packed minced cilantro
¼ cup chopped canned green chiles
1 tablespoon rice vinegar
2 teaspoons freshly squeezed lime juice

Flan

MAKES 6 SCANT ½-CUP SERVINGS

Besides being delicious as a dessert, leftover flan, served with fresh fruit, makes a wonderful breakfast treat. This version takes less than an hour from start to finish—and it's fabulous.

1. Preheat oven to 250° F. Put all ingredients in a blender and blend well.

2. Pour mixture into a 6-cup baking dish or 6 individual ramekins and sprinkle generously with cinnamon.

3. Set baking dish in oven (if using ramekins, place them on a baking sheet for easier handling) and bake about 1 hour, or until set. May be served warm, at room temperature, or cold. To reheat, place individual servings in a microwave for about 30 seconds, or until flan warms to room temperature. Be careful to not overheat or the flan will liquify and separate.

Each serving contains approximately:
113 calories, 2 g fat, 74 mg cholesterol, 173 mg sodium

2 eggs
3 egg whites
½ cup low-fat milk
1 can (12 oz) evaporated nonfat milk
3 tablespoons sugar
½ teaspoon ground cinnamon
¼ teaspoon ground nutmeg
⅛ teaspoon salt
1 teaspoon vanilla extract
½ teaspoon maple extract
Ground cinnamon, for garnish

MAKE-BELIEVE MARGARITAS

MAKES 2 MARGARITAS

1 cup bottled Margarita mix

⅓ cup water, very cold

1 tablespoon freshly squeezed lime juice

½ cup crushed ice

Lime slices, for garnish (optional)

For a fiesta drink the whole family can enjoy, try these nonalcoholic Margaritas.

1. Combine all ingredients in a blender and blend until frothy. Pour into glasses and garnish with a slice of lime, if desired.

TIP:

Dress up your Make-Believe Margaritas with an authentic presentation: Rub the rim of a chilled glass with a lime wedge. Then dip the rim of the glass into a dish of coarse salt and turn gently, encrusting the rim with salt. Pour the margarita into the prepared glass and serve at once.

Each serving contains approximately:
50 calories, no fat, no cholesterol, 20 mg sodium

HELP!
COMPANY'S
COMING

SERVES 4

Artichoke Antipasto With
Roasted Red Peppers

Linguine With Herbed Clam Sauce

Roasted Garlic Spread With French Bread

Marsala Poached Pears

Italian Chardonnay
or Mineral Water

This is one of my favorite "emergency" meals for those occasions
when company's coming for dinner and you've no time to shop
and only a little time to prepare.
Keep all the ingredients for this
menu on hand in your '90s-Style
Pantry (see page 147) and you
will always be able to create a
healthy, light meal in minutes for
your family and guests.

ARTICHOKE ANTIPASTO WITH ROASTED RED PEPPERS

MAKES FOUR ¾-CUP SERVINGS

MARINADE:

1 tablespoon red wine vinegar

½ teaspoon balsamic vinegar

⅛ teaspoon salt

¼ teaspoon sugar

⅛ teaspoon freshly ground
    black pepper

¼ teaspoon dried oregano,
    crushed

⅛ teaspoon Dijon-style mustard

1 garlic clove, pressed or minced

1 tablespoon extra virgin olive oil

1 can (8½ oz) quartered
    artichoke hearts, drained

1 jar (7 oz) roasted red peppers,

Quick and easy to make, this colorful, luscious antipasto relies totally on ingredients from the pantry.

1. To make marinade, combine vinegars, salt, and sugar and stir until dissolved. Add all other ingredients and mix well.

2. Combine drained artichoke hearts and red peppers in a bowl and mix well. Add marinade and toss until red peppers start to break apart and dressing turns red, about 1 minute.

3. Serve at once or refrigerate, covered, for several hours or overnight. Serve at room temperature.

Each serving contains approximately:
69 calories, 4 g fat, no cholesterol, 34 mg sodium

LINGUINE WITH HERBED CLAM SAUCE

MAKES FOUR 1¼-CUP SERVINGS

This is a really quick and easy dish. Just remember, do not boil the clams as it will make them very tough and chewy. Serve with warm bread and roasted garlic (see Timesaver Tip).

1. Cook pasta according to package directions. It should be al dente (see Tip on page 5). Drain and keep warm.

2. Drain clams and pour juice into saucepan. Add garlic and oregano and bring to a boil.

3. Remove from heat and add clams, stirring gently to heat them through.

4. Toss pasta with clam mixture and grated Parmesan cheese.

Each serving contains approximately:
293 calories, 7 g fat, 105 mg cholesterol, 371 mg sodium

drained
¾ pound dry linguine (4 cups cooked)
1 garlic clove, minced or pressed
¼ teaspoon dried oregano, crushed
2 cans (8 oz each) chopped clams, undrained
2 ounces imported Parmesan cheese, grated (½ cup)

TIP:
Buy plenty of fine imported Parmesan or Romano cheeses—especially if the price is good—and keep on hand in the refrigerator. A little bit goes a long way toward transforming ordinary dishes into gourmet food. Always save the tough outer rind of cheeses to add extra flavor to soup and stews. Remove pieces of rind before serving.

TIMESAVER TIP:
Buy a tube of roasted garlic spread and keep in the refrigerator. It makes a full-flavored accompaniment to a crusty Italian or French bread you've pulled from the freezer.

Marsala Poached Pears

MAKES FOUR ½-CUP SERVINGS

1 can (16 oz) pears packed
in juice
¼ cup Marsala

You won't believe how such a fast and simple dessert can be so delicious. For the best flavor, use a good-quality Marsala wine.

1. Drain pears and pour juice into saucepan. Add Marsala to juice and bring slowly to a boil over low heat.

2. Turn off heat, add pears, and cover pan. Allow pears to steep in Marsala and juice mixture until ready to serve.

3. Divide pears among 4 serving dishes; pour sauce over them. Serve at room temperature.

TIP:
Keep purchased or homemade biscotti (see page 49) on hand to serve as a delightful accompaniment for a simple dessert such as these poached pears. Biscotti also go well with coffee, tea, or wine.

Each serving contains approximately:
93 calories, no fat, no cholesterol, 7 mg sodium

SWORDFISH ON SEAWEED

SERVES 4

Red Pepper Soup

Swordfish on Seaweed With
Broccoli and Pine Nuts

Mystery Pilaf

Prune and Armagnac Ice "Cream"

Dry White Wine or Mineral Water

*Steaming fish or other foods on
a bed of seaweed is a technique
I learned at the Ritz Cooking
School in Paris. I've used it ever
since because it makes such a
dramatic presentation and keeps
the fish moist and flavorful.*

RED PEPPER SOUP

MAKES FOUR ¾-CUP SERVINGS

1½ tablespoons extra virgin olive oil

1 small onion, finely chopped
   (1 cup)

4 large red bell peppers, seeds
   and membranes removed,
   chopped (4 cups)

½ teaspoon salt (omit if using
   salted stock)

½ teaspoon freshly ground
   black pepper

2 cups defatted Chicken Stock
   (see page 88)

¼ cup nonfat yogurt, for garnish

TIP:
This soup makes a colorful, tasty
sauce for fish, poultry, meat, or
pasta.

*Gorgeous, delicious, healthy, unusual, and easy to make! For this
menu it's served hot, although it is good cold or at room temperature as
well. Yellow peppers will also work in this recipe but make the soup
less colorful.*

1. Heat oil in a large pot. Add onion and cook until soft, about 5 to
   10 minutes; do not brown. Add red peppers, salt, and pepper,
   and cook 5 more minutes.

2. Add chicken stock and bring to a boil. Reduce heat and simmer,
   uncovered, for 15 minutes. Allow to cool about 5 minutes. Pour
   half the mixture into a blender and purée, being careful to vent
   the blender lid. Repeat with remaining mixture. Pour through a
   sieve or strainer and heat to serving temperature.

3. Garnish with a dollop of yogurt.

TIP:
For a fancy presentation, garnish the soup with an overlapping leaf
design of yogurt. Fill a plastic squeeze bottle with plain nonfat yogurt blended smooth with a fork or whisk. Squeeze two silver
dollar–sized circles of yogurt onto the surface of the soup. Run the
blade of a knife or toothpick through the center of both circles, making a continuous line to form the midrib of the yogurt "leaves."

Each serving contains approximately:
100 calories, 6 g fat, no cholesterol, 338 mg sodium

SWORDFISH ON SEAWEED WITH BROCCOLI AND PINE NUTS

MAKES 4 SERVINGS

You can substitute any firm white fish for the swordfish. Dried seaweed is available in any Asian market and in many supermarkets.

1. Put dried seaweed in a large bowl and cover with water. Set aside.

2. Soak raisins in warm water to cover for 30 minutes, then drain and pat dry. While raisins are soaking, toast pine nuts in a skillet until golden brown, about 3 minutes (see Tip). Watch carefully; they burn easily. Set aside.

3. Clean and prepare broccoli florets, place in a steamer basket over rapidly boiling water, and steam 3 to 5 minutes. Immediately rinse under cold running water to intensify color. Drain thoroughly.

4. Heat olive oil and ¼ teaspoon salt in a large saucepan over medium heat. Add broccoli and raisins and cook, stirring, until broccoli is thoroughly heated. Add toasted pine nuts and toss lightly. Set aside.

5. Cut swordfish steaks into 2-inch pieces and sprinkle each with lemon juice, salt, and white pepper. Place reconstituted seaweed in a steamer basket over boiling water. Place fish on top of seaweed, cover, and steam for about 5 minutes, or until the fish turns from translucent to opaque. Do not overcook.

6. To serve, place a mound of the broccoli and pine nut mixture in the center of each plate and arrange 4 fish medallions on top. Garnish with a few strands of seaweed used in the steamer.

TIP:
To toast pine nuts, place in a cold skillet over moderately low heat and shake skillet constantly so that they color evenly. Remove immediately when they turn golden brown.

Each serving contains approximately:
476 calories, 14 g fat, 64 mg cholesterol, 715 mg sodium

1 package (2 oz) dried seaweed

½ cup raisins
2 tablespoons pine nuts, toasted
2 pounds broccoli florets
1 tablespoon extra virgin olive oil
¼ teaspoon salt

1½ pounds swordfish steaks
2 tablespoons freshly squeezed
   lemon juice
   Salt
   White pepper

TIP:
Pine nuts become rancid very quickly, so buy them in small amounts and store them in the refrigerator.

MYSTERY PILAF

MAKES 4 CUPS, EIGHT ½-CUP SERVINGS

½ cup uncooked vermicelli,
  broken into 1-inch pieces

1 tablespoon corn oil

1 cup uncooked long-grain
  white rice

½ medium onion, thinly sliced
  (1 cup)

2 tablespoons low-sodium
  soy sauce

1 teaspoon dried thyme, crushed

2 cups defatted Chicken Stock
  (see page 88)

The toasted vermicelli is the "mystery" in this dish, since few people can figure out what it is.

1. Preheat oven to 400° F. Place vermicelli on a cookie sheet with sides or in a baking dish. Bake, stirring occasionally, until vermicelli is a rich brown color.

2. In a heavy skillet over medium heat, warm oil. Add rice and onion and cook, stirring frequently, until mixture is thoroughly browned.

3. In a pot combine browned vermicelli, soy sauce, thyme, and stock and bring to a boil. Transfer rice mixture to a casserole with a tight-fitting lid. Add stock mixture, stir, cover, and bake 40 minutes. Remove from oven and allow to stand 10 minutes before removing lid.

Each serving contains approximately:
148 calories, 3 g fat, no cholesterol, 155 mg sodium

PRUNE AND ARMAGNAC ICE "CREAM"

MAKES ONE PINT, FOUR ½-CUP SERVINGS

1 pint vanilla ice milk, slightly
  softened

4 plump, moist, pitted prunes,
  finely chopped

1½ tablespoons Armagnac or other
  brandy

TIP:
Prunes and other dried fruits are easier to chop finely if you first freeze them until they are firm.

The first time I tasted a dessert similar to this one was many years ago in a little bistro in the south of France.

1. Combine ice milk, prunes, and Armagnac in a bowl and mix thoroughly. Spoon mixture back into ice milk carton and freeze until firm.

VARIATIONS:
Make your own varieties of ice "cream" by adding different flavorings. My own favorites are peanut butter, baked apple, and amaretto.

Each serving contains approximately:
165 calories, 2 g fat, 7 mg cholesterol, 82 mg sodium

THE EMERGENCY GOURMET

SERVES 6

Antipasto Salad

Cioppino

San Francisco Sourdough French Bread

Fresh Fruit

Dry White Wine or Mineral Water

You *can pull this San Francisco specialty together in minutes from "emergency" ingredients you've stored ahead in your '90s-Style Pantry, which incorporates cupboards, refrigerator, and freezer (see page 147). And for those rare times when there's no emergency, I've also included a classic sourdough bread recipe.*

ANTIPASTO SALAD

MAKES SIX 1½-CUP SERVINGS

DRESSING:

½ teaspoon balsamic vinegar

¼ teaspoon salt

1 tablespoon dry red wine

⅛ teaspoon dry mustard

¼ teaspoon sugar

Dash of freshly ground black pepper

⅛ teaspoon dried basil, crushed

⅛ teaspoon dried tarragon, crushed

⅛ teaspoon dried oregano, crushed

2 tablespoons extra virgin olive oil

SALAD:

1 ounce (¼ cup packed) sun-dried tomatoes

8 cups assorted salad greens, torn in bite-size pieces

¼ cup freshly grated Parmesan cheese

1 can (16 oz) caponata (Mediterranean-style eggplant)

1 can (15–16 oz) canned garbanzos (chick-peas), drained

½ cup diced part-skim mozzarella cheese

Edible flowers, for garnish (optional)

One of my favorite summer supper entrées is this lush salad, accompanied by a loaf of crusty Italian or sourdough bread.

1. Combine vinegar and salt, stirring until salt is dissolved. Add all other dressing ingredients except oil and mix thoroughly. Slowly add oil, stirring constantly. Set aside.

2. Using a knife or kitchen scissors, cut tomatoes into thin strips and put them in a small bowl. Cover with boiling water and allow to stand for 2 minutes. Drain and set aside.

3. Toss salad greens with Parmesan cheese. Add drained tomatoes and all remaining salad ingredients and mix well. Add dressing and toss thoroughly. Garnish as desired with edible flowers.

Each serving contains approximately:
288 calories, 12 g fat, 8 mg cholesterol, 557 mg sodium

CIOPPINO

MAKES 6 SERVINGS

San Francisco, not Italy, is the birthplace of cioppino. The dish is the creation of Italian sailors who traveled to the West Coast during the Gold Rush. They combined the local shellfish with their own spicy marinara-style sauce to make what has become a world-renowned stew. This dish makes for delicious but messy eating, so offer your guests bibs and plenty of extra napkins, as well as bowls to hold the discarded shells.

1. In a large pot, combine onion, green onions, bell pepper, and garlic. Cook covered over very low heat until onion is clear but not browned, about 10 minutes.

2. Add tomato purée, tomato sauce, clam juice, wine and all seasonings. Cover and simmer over very low heat for one hour.

3. Add crab and shrimp. Cook, covered, until shrimp turns pink, about 5 minutes. Remove and discard shrimp heads. Return shrimp and add steamed clams.

TIP:
Cook the clams separately to avoid overcooking the rest of the shellfish. Steam clams until the shells open and then add them to the finished stew. Discard any unopened clams.

MAKE-AHEAD TIP:
The sauce base for cioppino can be prepared up to the point of adding the shellfish and then frozen until you want a quick gourmet meal. Thaw the sauce, reheat, add fresh shellfish and cook just until done.

Each serving contains approximately:
281 calories, 3 g fat, 213 mg cholesterol, 1928 mg sodium

1 large onion, chopped (2 cups)

8 green onions (tops included), chopped

1 green bell pepper, seeds and membranes removed, chopped

2 garlic cloves, pressed or finely chopped

1 can (16 oz) tomato purée

1 can (8 oz) tomato sauce

1 cup clam juice

1 cup dry white wine

1 bay leaf

1/8 teaspoon dried rosemary, crushed

1/4 teaspoon dried thyme, crushed

1/2 teaspoon dried oregano, crushed

1/2 teaspoon salt

1/4 teaspoon freshly ground black pepper

2 medium crabs, cracked and broken into pieces

1 pound large shrimp or prawns in the shells, cleaned and deveined

12 clams in the shells, scrubbed and steamed until open

TIP:
Instead of sautéing onions and pepper in butter, margarine, or oil, you can reduce fat and calories by gently cooking them in a heavy pan over very low heat. If your pan isn't heavy, add a small amount of water to prevent scorching as the onions cook in their own juices.

PREPARING SHRIMP

1. Remove legs. Peel a bit of shell from head end of body. Holding the peeled section with hand, pull tail with other hand and shell will come off. If you wish to leave shell and tail intact, use scissors to slit shell on back of body so that you can remove the vein.

2. Slit shrimp down outside curve and remove the intestinal vein, if there is one. On larger shrimp the intestinal vein contains undesirable grit, but on some medium shrimp the vein is not present.

SAN FRANCISCO SOURDOUGH FRENCH BREAD

MAKES TWO 16-INCH LONG LOAVES OR 12-INCH ROUND LOAVES, OR FOUR BAGUETTES, APPROXIMATELY THIRTY-TWO SERVINGS

1 cup sourdough starter (see page 79)

3 cups warm (105° F to 115° F) water

6½ to 7 cups unbleached bread flour

1 tablespoon salt
Oil, for greasing

1 package active dry yeast
Cornmeal, for dusting

1 egg, beaten with ¼ cup milk or water (optional)

TIMESAVER TIP:
When you can't make your own, buy sourdough bread from a good bakery.

Save this classic recipe for some relaxing weekend when you have the time to let the dough ferment and rise at the leisurely pace it needs to become really sour. The flavor and aroma of your own freshly baked sourdough bread makes it worth your while to make it yourself. And, you can freeze a loaf or two for the next time there's an emergency!

1. Two nights before you plan to bake the bread, follow the procedure in Step 1 for making Sourdough Starter (recipe follows), adding 2½ cups of the warm water and 2½ cups of the flour to the 1 cup of starter. Let mixture sit 8 to 12 hours.

2. The next day return 1 cup sponge to storage container. To remaining sponge add salt and 2½ cups flour. Stir until dough is too stiff to work. Spread 1 cup flour on board, turn out dough onto board, and knead until dough is smooth and resilient, 8 to 10 minutes. Add more flour as necessary to keep dough from sticking; knead until flour is thoroughly incorporated.

3. Place dough ball in lightly oiled bowl and turn to oil all surfaces. Cover bowl with plastic wrap and let rise 4 to 6 hours in a warm place. Punch down dough, cover again, and refrigerate overnight.

4. On the day of baking, remove dough from refrigerator and allow to return to room temperature. In a large bowl warmed with hot water, dissolve yeast in ½ cup of the warm water. Add dough and knead to incorporate yeast mixture. Add ½ cup flour and knead in bowl until surface is not too sticky, then turn dough out onto a floured surface and knead until smooth, adding additional flour as needed.

5. Return dough to oiled bowl and let rise, covered, until doubled in bulk, about 1 hour. Punch down and let rise again if time allows; otherwise, proceed to form loaves.

6. Preheat oven to 350° F. Punch down dough after rising. Form into 2 loaves or 4 baguettes and place on baking sheets dusted with cornmeal; allow room between loaves for rising. Cover with a towel and let dough rise about 45 minutes, or until nearly doubled in bulk. If desired, brush tops lightly with egg mixture. Slash tops, making shallow cuts with a sharp knife or razor blade (lengthwise or diagonally on long loaves, crosshatched on round loaves). Bake on lowest shelf of oven about 1 hour, or until crust is golden brown and loaves sound hollow when tapped on bottom. Cool on racks.

Each serving contains approximately:
68 calories, negligible fat, negligible cholesterol, 145 mg sodium

SOURDOUGH STARTER:

You will need either a commercially packaged dry starter mix or a cup of borrowed homemade starter from someone who keeps a batch going. If you are using a dry starter mix, prepare it according to package directions. Most starters require several days to establish, so plan ahead.

1. Combine starter and the water in a large bowl. Stir in flour and beat to a smooth batter.

2. Cover bowl with plastic wrap and set aside in a warm (about 75° F) place. Let mixture stand until bubbly and sour, and a clear liquid begins to collect on surface (6 to 12 hours, depending on liveliness of starter.

3. Stir starter, scoop out 1 cup of sponge, and place it in glass or ceramic storage container; refrigerate until next use.

SOURDOUGH STARTER:

1 cup sourdough starter (from a packaged mix or homemade)
Equal parts warm (105° F to 115° F) water and unbleached bread flour (at least 1 cup each)

MENUS WITH POULTRY

MENUS WITH POULTRY

Chicken and the white meat of turkey closely follow fish as desirable sources of protein in a healthy diet. Unlike the fat in red meat, which is spread throughout the red muscle of the meat, poultry fat is concentrated in or just below the skin and therefore easily removed. Besides being relatively low in fat, poultry is one of the most versatile of foods: It can appear on the table in a multitude of forms, including such dishes as Red Pepper Soup (page 72) made with Chicken Stock (page 88), Poultry Potstickers With Gingered Orange Sauce (page 98), and Paillard of Chicken (page 105).

THAI COUNTRY COOKING

SERVES 6

Tom Koong (Shrimp Soup)

Cucumber and Peanut Salad

Som Kai Thai Thai
(Country-Style Chicken Curry)

Jasmine Rice or White Rice

Baked Papaya With "Coconut" Sauce

Thai Beer or Nonalcoholic Beer

The difference between city and country cooking in Thailand centers largely on the use of a single ingredient—coconut milk. In Thai city, or royal, cuisine it is a common ingredient, but in the country it is rarely used. Because coconut is the most highly saturated of all fats, Thai country cooking tends to be healthier and lighter than its urban counterpart.

TOM KOONG
(SHRIMP SOUP)

MAKES SIX 1-CUP SERVINGS

5 cups defatted Chicken Stock (see page 88)

1 daikon (12 oz), peeled and diced (3 cups)

¾ pound shrimp, peeled and deveined

1 tablespoon palm sugar or light brown sugar

3 tablespoons fish sauce or soy sauce

1 teaspoon chili paste

1 tablespoon rice vinegar
Cilantro, for garnish

Using authentic ingredients makes all the difference in this recipe, which I acquired when attending the Thai Cooking School in the Oriental Hotel in Bangkok. Most supermarket produce sections carry daikon, which resembles a large white radish, although you may need to visit an Asian market to find palm sugar, fish sauce, and chili paste.

1. In a large pot bring chicken stock to a boil. Add daikon and cook until translucent and easily pierced with a fork, about 10 minutes.

2. Add shrimp and cook until pink, about 2 minutes.

3. Add all remaining ingredients, except cilantro, and mix well. Ladle into bowls and garnish with cilantro.

Each serving contains approximately:
97 calories, 1 g fat, 111 mg cholesterol, 1117 mg sodium.

CUCUMBER AND PEANUT SALAD

MAKES SIX ¾-CUP SERVINGS

1 cup rice vinegar

4 tablespoons sugar

2 teaspoons salt

4 tablespoons chopped red chiles, or to taste

1 cup chopped shallots

4 cups sliced cucumbers

4 tablespoons chopped peanuts

4 tablespoons chopped cilantro
Green onions, for garnish (optional)

Although the red chiles used in this popular side dish are a common ingredient in Thai cuisine, chiles are not indigenous to Thailand. They were introduced by the Portuguese, who brought them from South America. This salad can be made fiery by adding more red chiles or cooled down by replacing them with red bell peppers.

1. Combine vinegar, sugar, and salt in a saucepan. Cook over low heat, stirring constantly, until sugar and salt are completely dissolved. Remove from heat and cool to room temperature.

2. Combine vinegar mixture with chiles, shallots, cucumbers, and peanuts and mix well. Top with cilantro and garnish with a green onion, if desired. Serve immediately to prevent the cucumber from becoming soft.

Each serving contains approximately:
113 calories, 3 g fat, no cholesterol, 815 mg sodium

Som Kai Thai Thai
(Country-Style Chicken Curry)

MAKES SIX 1-CUP SERVINGS

Visit a Thai or Asian market for the chili paste, lemongrass, Kaffir lime leaves, galangal, and fish sauce for this dish from the Thai Cooking School in Bangkok.

1. In a food processor combine chili paste, garlic, shallots, lemongrass, lime leaves, and galangal and process until smooth.

2. Bring chicken stock to a rapid boil. Add blended mixture and stir constantly until slightly thickened. Add lime juice, fish sauce, and palm sugar and mix well while mixture continues to boil.

3. Add cubed chicken and cook, stirring constantly, until chicken turns from translucent to opaque, about 3 to 4 minutes. Add steamed vegetables and immediately remove from heat.

4. Serve with cooked rice.

MAKE-AHEAD TIP:

If you want to make the curry a day or so in advance, follow the recipe but omit the steamed vegetables. Cool the curry and refrigerate it. Then, while you're reheating the curry, lightly steam the vegetables and add them at the last minute so they'll retain their crisp-tender texture.

Each serving contains approximately:
95 calories, 2 g fat, 125 mg cholesterol, 785 mg sodium

1 tablespoon chili paste

4 garlic cloves, minced or pressed

6 shallots, minced

1 tablespoon sliced lemongrass

1 teaspoon finely chopped Kaffir lime leaves

3 tablespoons minced galangal (Thai ginger) or peeled, minced fresh ginger

2 cups Chicken Stock (see page 88)

⅓ cup freshly squeezed lime juice

¼ cup fish sauce

1 teaspoon palm sugar or light brown sugar

3 chicken breast halves, skinned, boned, and cubed

3 cups mixed vegetables (cauliflower, green beans, snow peas, squash, eggplant, baby corn, spinach, etc.), steamed just until crisp-tender

Cooked jasmine or white rice

TIP:

Adding a stalk of lemongrass to rice and other Asian dishes as they are cooking lends a subtle citrus flavor and aroma. If you can't find lemongrass in your area, a piece of lemon rind makes a good substitute. Remember to remove it before serving.

Baked Papaya With "Coconut" Sauce

Sauce:

¾ cup melted vanilla ice milk

½ teaspoon coconut extract

3 ripe papayas

⅓ cup honey

1 tablespoon finely chopped fresh ginger

Tip:

To achieve the taste of coconut milk without the undesirable saturated fat, flavor any milk product with a small amount of coconut extract.

The sweetness of this dessert balances the spiciness and saltiness typical of other Thai menu components. The creamy, rich "coconut" sauce demonstrates one of my favorite tricks for cooking light. Melting vanilla ice milk and flavoring it with extracts or liqueurs works well as a sauce in many recipes (see Variations on page 6).

1. To make sauce, combine melted ice milk and coconut extract. Mix well and set aside.

2. Preheat oven to 350° F. Cut papayas in half lengthwise and remove seeds. Combine honey and ginger and mix well. Spread 1 tablespoon of the honey-ginger mixture on each papaya half.

3. Place the papaya halves, cut side up, in a baking dish and bake about 30 minutes, or until lightly browned.

4. Top each serving with 2 tablespoons sauce. Serve warm.

Each serving contains approximately:
92 calories, 1 g fat, 4 mg cholesterol, 13 mg sodium

CHICKEN MAGIC

CHICKEN STOCK COMES FULL CIRCLE

SERVES 8

Sautéed Chicken Breast

Broccoli Stars

Whole Wheat Bread
or Baguettes

Grand Marnier Soufflé

Chardonnay or Pinot Noir

The magic in this menu is using
the chicken stock to replace the
fat in sautéing. An old vegetable
favorite in a new guise and a bil-
lowing dessert fit for royalty
round out the menu.

SAUTÉED CHICKEN BREAST

MAKES 8 SERVINGS

8 frozen cubes (or about 1 cup)
chicken stock, as needed
(recipe follows)
8 chicken breast halves, skinned
and boned

One of the best ways to lighten cuisine is by lowering the fat content. One of the best substitutes for fat is glace, made by reducing defatted stock to a rich, flavorful concentrate. Although this recipe features chicken breasts, virtually any food, including vegetables, will glaze beautifully using this method.

1. Put 2 of the stock cubes (or ¼ cup stock) in a large sauté pan or skillet. Reduce over medium heat until pan is glazed. Add 2 chicken breasts and cook about 2 minutes per side, or until nicely browned and firm to the touch. Add a little more of the stock as needed to prevent scorching. Overcooking will cause the chicken to toughen. Repeat with remaining breast halves.

Each serving contains approximately:
148 calories, 3 g fat, 80 mg cholesterol, 70 mg sodium

CHICKEN STOCK

MAKES APPROXIMATELY 10 CUPS

3 to 5 pounds chicken bones
and parts
2 carrots, peeled and cut
into pieces
2 celery ribs, without leaves,
cut into pieces
1 onion, unpeeled and quartered
2 to 4 garlic cloves, unpeeled
and halved
3 parsley sprigs
1 bay leaf
12 peppercorns
¼ cup vinegar

Your own homemade stock is both tastier and far more economical than the canned variety. If you don't have enough chicken carcasses and scraps on hand, buy wings, backs, and necks—all inexpensively priced and ideal for making stock. Keep in mind that making your own chicken stock takes only 15 minutes of actual preparation time.

1. Put all ingredients into a large pot with a lid. Add cold water to cover by at least 3 inches and bring slowly to a simmer.

2. Reduce heat and cover pot, leaving lid ajar. Simmer at least 3 hours. (The longer you cook the stock, the more flavorful it will be.)

3. Remove pot from heat. Remove and discard chicken and vegetables, which by this point will have lost all their flavor and nutritional value. Strain stock and cool slightly before refrigerating.

4. To defat stock, refrigerate, uncovered, several hours or overnight, until all the fat congeals on top. With a rubber spatula or spoon, remove fat and discard.

5. Pour defatted stock into the size containers you use most frequently. Seal tightly. Frozen chicken stock will keep its flavor for several months if it is sealed in airtight containers.

TIP:

Ice-cube trays are ideal for freezing stock you plan to use for glace. When the stock has frozen into cubes, remove from trays, place in zip-top plastic bags, and store in the freezer until needed. Each cube equals 2 tablespoons of stock.

TIMESAVER TIP:

Even when there's no time to make your own stock, you'll never be without if you keep a few cans of chicken stock in the refrigerator. When you need some defatted stock for a recipe, simply open a can and remove and discard the congealed fat before using. Just remember to replenish your supply of canned refrigerated stock every time you use it up.

Each cup contains:
negligible calories, negligible fat, negligible cholesterol, negligible sodium

NOTE: Nutritional value of the stock will vary according to the exact amount of ingredients used and the length of cooking time.

TIP:

When making stock, peel the carrots (but not the onions and garlic) and remove the celery leaves. The exterior surface of the carrot peel oxidizes, tending to make the stock bitter, as do the celery leaves. The onions and garlic are left unpeeled because the skins do not affect the flavor of the stock and they also add some color.

BROCCOLI STARS

MAKES EIGHT ½-CUP SERVINGS

Ever wish somebody would come up with a "new" vegetable? The good news is that you can do it yourself, using a part of the broccoli that many people throw away. Slice across a stalk of broccoli, and you will see that each slice has a star pattern, which gives this dish its name.

1. Slice broccoli stalks crosswise into ¼-inch-thick stars. If you have a food processor, by all means use it to achieve thin, even slices.

2. In a large saucepan steam stars over rapidly boiling water until they are crisp-tender, 3 to 4 minutes. Remove from heat and rinse under cold running water. Drain thoroughly. Serve hot or chilled.

Each serving contains approximately:
23 calories, no fat, no cholesterol, 9 mg sodium

6 to 8 broccoli stalks (1 lb)

TIP:

Broccoli stars are just as nutritious and versatile as broccoli florets. They're great fun to serve because few people will know what they are and, since the stalks are ordinarily discarded, they are economical.

GRAND MARNIER SOUFFLÉ

SAUCE:

1 cup melted vanilla ice milk

1½ teaspoons Grand Marnier

SOUFFLÉ:

2 tablespoons corn oil margarine

2½ tablespoons unbleached flour

1 can (12 oz) evaporated nonfat milk, at the boiling point

2 egg yolks

⅓ cup sugar

3 tablespoons Grand Marnier

2 teaspoons vanilla extract

6 egg whites

⅛ teaspoon salt

⅛ teaspoon cream of tartar

An incredibly easy, sensational-tasting sauce makes the "Queen of soufflés" truly regal and truly light!

1. To make sauce, combine melted ice milk and Grand Marnier and mix well. Cover and set aside.

2. Melt margarine in a large saucepan over medium heat. Add flour and stir constantly for 2 minutes, being careful not to brown. Remove from heat and add scalded milk, all at once, stirring with a wire whisk. Reduce heat to low and return pan to stove. Bring to a boil and simmer until thickened. Remove from heat and add egg yolks, one at a time, stirring each one in thoroughly. Add sugar, Grand Marnier, and vanilla. Mix well and set aside.

3. Preheat oven to 400° F. In a large mixing bowl beat egg whites until frothy. Add salt and cream of tartar and continue beating until stiff but not dry. Stir one third of the egg whites into sauce mixture. Gently fold the remaining egg whites into the mixture, being careful not to overmix.

4. Pour mixture into an 8-inch soufflé dish and place it in the center of the oven. Immediately reduce temperature to 375° F. Cook about 20 minutes, or until soufflé billows and is lightly browned.

5. Spoon 2 tablespoons sauce over each serving and serve immediately.

Each serving contains approximately:
163 calories, 5 g fat, 54 mg cholesterol, 149 mg sodium

FRENCH BISTRO COOKING

SERVES 8

Salad of Mixed Greens With Roquefort Dressing and Toasted Walnuts

Chicken Stew Provençal With Light Aioli

Whole Wheat Baguettes

Cherry Berry Clafoutis

French Chablis

The warm, unpretentious ambiance of France's bistros have long attracted tourists and natives alike. The repertoire of bistro classics is typically economical and wholesome, incorporating fresh seasonal produce, dried legumes, grains, less expensive cuts of poultry and meat, and every kind of leftover imaginable. The reduced fat and cholesterol in this traditional bistro fare make these dishes satisfying and healthy.

SALAD OF MIXED GREENS WITH ROQUEFORT DRESSING AND TOASTED WALNUTS

MAKES 8 SERVINGS

DRESSING:

1 cup buttermilk

½ cup silken-soft tofu

3 ounces Roquefort cheese (about ⅓ cup, packed)

1½ teaspoons canola or corn oil

1½ teaspoons freshly squeezed lemon juice

1 garlic clove, quartered

½ teaspoon salt

¼ teaspoon freshly ground black pepper

¼ cup low-fat cottage cheese

32 walnut halves

8 cups assorted greens (Belgian endive, romaine, radicchio, watercress, Bibb lettuce, arugula, etc.)

You can make this salad hours ahead of serving time, plate it, cover it with plastic wrap, and refrigerate it. And if you generally avoid Roquefort dressings because they're typically higher in calories, cholesterol, and sodium than any other dressing, this is one for you. It's easy to make, tastes fabulous, and keeps for several days in the refrigerator. In fact, it's best to chill for 24 hours.

1. To make dressing, combine all ingredients in a blender and blend until smooth.

2. Refrigerate in a tightly covered container for at least 24 hours before using to allow flavors to blend.

3. Preheat oven to 350° F. Place walnut halves in a pan on the center rack of oven and bake for 8 to 10 minutes, or until lightly toasted. Watch them carefully, as they burn easily. Set aside. (Nuts can also be toasted in a toaster oven or dry skillet.)

4. Arrange greens on individual chilled plates. To serve, spoon 2 tablespoons dressing over each plate. Garnish each serving with 4 toasted walnut halves.

Each serving contains approximately:
59 calories, 6 g fat, 7 mg cholesterol, 227 mg sodium

CHICKEN STEW PROVENÇAL WITH LIGHT AIOLI

MAKES 8 SERVINGS

This is the entrée I demonstrated when teaching a cooking class at the D'Gustibus Cooking School at Macy's in New York, and it received rave reviews. It is an all-time bistro classic that happens to be my favorite recipe for spur-of-the-moment entertaining.

1. In a large pot or soup kettle, combine fennel, onions, canned tomatoes and their juice, garlic, bay leaves, thyme, salt, and peppers and mix well. Cover and slowly bring to a boil. Reduce heat and simmer 30 minutes.

2. Add chicken thighs, burying them in the mixture so they will absorb the flavor of the other ingredients as they cook. Continue to simmer, covered, 30 more minutes.

3. Add potatoes and chicken stock and cook until potatoes can be easily pierced with a fork, about 10 to 15 minutes. Add the liqueur and simmer, covered, 30 more minutes.

4. To serve, spoon approximately 2 cups stew and 2 chicken thighs into each of eight large bowls. Top with a dollop of Light Aioli.

MAKE-AHEAD TIP:
You can make this dish ahead through Step 3, refrigerate it in a covered container, and reheat it shortly before the meal is ready. Top with the Light Aioli just before serving.

Each serving contains approximately:
295 calories, 15 g fat, negligible cholesterol, 197 mg sodium

2 fennel bulbs (fronds included), coarsely chopped (8 cups)

4 medium onions, coarsely chopped (6 cups)

1 can (28 oz) Italian plum tomatoes

4 garlic cloves, pressed or minced

2 bay leaves

½ teaspoon chopped fresh thyme or ¼ teaspoon dried, crushed

½ teaspoon salt (omit if using salted stock)

½ teaspoon freshly ground black pepper

⅛ teaspoon cayenne pepper

16 chicken thighs, skinned and boned

8 medium potatoes, scrubbed and quartered (4 cups)

1½ cups defatted Chicken Stock (see page 88)

⅓ cup anise-flavored liqueur (such as Anisette or Pernod) Light Aioli (see page 94)

TIP:
If you're serving buffet-style and want to save your guests the trouble of having to use a knife to cut the chicken, substitute cubed chicken for the whole thighs.

LIGHT AIOLI

MAKES 1 CUP, EIGHT 2-TABLESPOON SERVINGS

1 cup (8 oz) silken-firm tofu

2 tablespoons freshly squeezed
lemon juice

2 tablespoons extra virgin
olive oil

3 large garlic cloves, minced

½ teaspoon salt

⅛ teaspoon freshly ground
black pepper

Don't let the first ingredient in this delicious recipe put you off. Try it—you'll like the authentic taste and texture and the fact that this version, unlike the "real" one, contains no cholesterol!

1. Combine all ingredients in a blender and blend until satin-smooth. This is also a wonderful spread for bread.

Each serving contains approximately:
54 calories, 5 g fat, no cholesterol, 150 mg sodium

Cherry Berry Clafoutis

CHERRY BERRY CLAFOUTIS

MAKES EIGHT 1-CUP SERVINGS

1⅓ cups nonfat milk

½ cup sugar

1 egg

3 egg whites

2 teaspoons vanilla extract

⅛ teaspoon salt

¾ cup unbleached all-purpose flour

1 pound frozen pitted, unsweetened cherries, thawed and thoroughly drained (1½ cups)

1 pound frozen unsweetened strawberries, thawed and thoroughly drained (1½ cups)

2 tablespoons confectioners' sugar
Confectioners' sugar, for garnish (optional)

TIP:

If you make this recipe with fresh fruit, be sure to press the fruit firmly into the measuring cup.

This fancy-sounding French dessert (see page 95) is actually an inexpensive, easy-to-make peasant dish that looks very much like a fruit tart. It can be made from almost any fresh, frozen, or canned fruit. I have used frozen cherries and strawberries in this recipe simply because they are available all year and require no preparation other than thawing and draining.

1. Preheat oven to 350° F. Spray entire inner surface of a 10-inch pie plate with nonstick vegetable coating and set aside. In a blender combine all ingredients expect the cherries, strawberries, and confectioners' sugar and blend on high speed for 1 minute.

2. Pour batter into pie plate and bake in center of oven 8 minutes. While batter is baking, in a bowl combine cherries and strawberries with confectioners' sugar and mix well. Remove pie plate from oven and spoon fruit mixture evenly over batter. To avoid spillovers, place pie plate on a baking sheet before carefully returning it to oven. Bake about 1 hour, or until puffed up and lightly browned.

3. Remove from oven and allow to cool at least 30 minutes before cutting. Sprinkle with confectioners' sugar, if desired. As the *clafoutis* cools it will lose some of its puffiness. Serve warm or at room temperature, by itself or topped with ice milk, frozen yogurt, Vanilla Cream (see page 20) or "Crème Anglaise" (see page 114).

Each serving contains approximately:
153 calories, 1 g fat, 27 mg cholesterol, 86 mg sodium

POULTRY POTSTICKERS

FOR POTLUCK STARDOM

SERVES 8

Egg Flower Soup

Poultry Potstickers
With Gingered Orange Sauce

Stir-Fried Sesame Asparagus

Sticky Black Rice Pudding

Champagne or Beer

Chinese food is certainly one of
the most popular ethnic cuisines
in North America, yet few people
ever try to make it themselves.
When was the last time you ate
homemade potstickers? If you
really want to impress someone
with your Asian cooking exper-
tise, serve this terrific menu.

EGG FLOWER SOUP

MAKES EIGHT ¾-CUP SERVINGS

6 cups Chicken Stock (see page 88)

2 eggs, well beaten

Chopped green onion tops, for garnish

Low-sodium soy sauce (optional)

Authentic taste and simple preparation make this low-fat, low-calorie soup almost too good to be true.

1. Bring chicken stock to a boil. Add beaten eggs, stirring constantly.

2. Continue stirring until eggs are cooked and stringy.

3. Garnish each serving with a sprinkle of the chopped green onion tops and add a few drops of low-sodium soy sauce, if desired.

Each serving contains approximately:
33 calories, 11 g fat, 59 mg cholesterol, 18 mg sodium

POULTRY POTSTICKERS WITH GINGERED ORANGE SAUCE

MAKES 24 POTSTICKERS

FILLING:

1 pound fresh spinach leaves, stems and large veins removed, chopped

1 egg white, lightly beaten

1 tablespoon low-sodium soy sauce

¼ teaspoon Chinese chili sauce

2 teaspoons peeled and minced fresh ginger

2 green onions (tops included), minced

½ pound ground chicken or turkey, cooked

These versatile potstickers are wonderful stuffed with poultry, meat, or vegetables. Using fresh spinach in the filling gives the best flavor and color.

1. Blanch spinach and drain thoroughly, squeezing out all moisture.

2. Combine egg white, soy sauce, chili sauce, ginger, and green onions; mix thoroughly. Add spinach and poultry, and mix again.

3. In a separate bowl, combine sauce ingredients and set aside.

4. Separate the wonton skins. Place 1 tablespoon filling onto each skin. Bring the 4 corners of each wonton skin into the center, overlapping to cover filling and form a ball. Place ball, folded side down, in the soft hollow of your hand between your thumb and index finger. Squeeze your hand together gently to form and seal each potsticker.

5. Place potsticker on a large baking sheet lightly dusted with cornstarch. Refrigerate uncovered for at least 1 hour before proceeding. (The recipe can be assembled several hours ahead to this point.)

6. Heat peanut oil in a large nonstick skillet over high heat. Add potstickers and cook until bottoms are golden brown. Turn each potsticker to brown the other side. Pour sauce over potstickers, cover, and steam for 3 minutes. Remove cover and continue cooking until all the sauce is absorbed.

7. Cut a V-shaped notch at both ends of the pea pods and arrange 3 in a spoke pattern on each of 8 plates. Place 3 potstickers on each of the plates between pea pods. Place an edible flower in the center of the plate.

Each potsticker contains approximately:
70 calories, 2 g fat, 13 mg cholesterol, 51 mg sodium

SAUCE:

½ cup water
1 tablespoon oyster sauce
½ teaspoon Chinese chili sauce
¼ teaspoon sugar
2 teaspoons grated orange zest
1 teaspoon peeled and minced fresh ginger

24 wonton skins
Cornstarch
2 tablespoons peanut oil
24 snow pea pods, strings removed and blanched, for garnish
8 edible flowers (pansies or nasturtiums), for garnish

TIMESAVER TIP:

When time is short you can replace the fresh spinach with two 10-ounce packages frozen spinach, thawed. Simply squeeze out the moisture; it doesn't need cooking.

FORMING POTSTICKERS

1. Place one tablespoon of filling in the center of each wonton wrapper. Fold each corner into the center, overlapping corners.

2. Press to seal.

3. Place the potsticker fold-side down in the soft hollow of your hand between thumb and forefinger. Squeeze your hand together gently to form a ball, holding it in place with the finger of your other hand.

4. This process also seals the bottom of the potsticker ball.

STIR-FRIED SESAME ASPARAGUS

MAKES EIGHT ½-CUP SERVINGS

Delicious with an Asian meal and equally wonderful as an addition to a Western-style tossed salad.

1. Cut off tough ends of asparagus and discard. Cut each spear diagonally into 1½-inch pieces.

2. Heat a frying pan until water sprinkled from your hand dances in the pan. Add sesame oil and tilt pan to coat the bottom. Add asparagus and stir-fry 2 to 3 minutes, or until it turns a very bright green.

Each serving contains approximately:
53 calories, 4 g fat, 53 mg cholesterol, 4 mg sodium

1¼ pounds asparagus
2 tablespoons dark sesame oil

TIP:
A member of the lily family, asparagus is at its best between March and June, when the fresh crop is harvested. Choose bright green spears that are brittle, not limp, with tightly closed tips, and stalks that are at least two-thirds green

To store, refrigerate the spears upright, with the stem ends in water; or wrap the cut ends in wet paper towels or cloth, cover with a plastic bag, and refrigerate for up to one week.

STICKY BLACK RICE PUDDING

1 cup sticky black (sweet) rice (available in Asian markets)

4 cups water

¼ cup nonfat milk

3 egg whites, lightly beaten

3 tablespoons sugar

1 tablespoon coconut extract

1 can (8 oz) water chestnuts, drained and diced

1 can (8 oz) crushed pineapple, drained

2 pounds mangoes, peeled, pitted, chopped, and puréed (2 cups)

8 edible flowers, for garnish

TIMESAVER TIP:

If there's no time to prepare the Sticky Black Rice Pudding, orange sherbet or sorbet is a refreshing alternative to serve with this menu.

If you can't find fresh mangoes, use fresh papaya or peaches (fresh, frozen, or canned in juice), or use your imagination and experiment!

1. Bring rice and water to a rapid boil. Continue to boil until all surface water has evaporated and top is covered with "craters." Reduce heat as low as possible and simmer, covered, for 20 minutes. Uncover and allow to cool to room temperature.

2. Combine rice with remaining ingredients except mango purée and flowers. Mix well.

3. Preheat oven to 325° F. Spoon rice mixture into a casserole and bake uncovered for 45 minutes. Remove from oven and allow to come to room temperature. Refrigerate until cold.

4. Strain mango purée and pour ¼ cup on each of 8 plates. Tilt each plate until purée covers the inner surface. Fill a ⅓-cup mold with rice pudding, pressing firmly, and unmold, using a spatula. Place molded pudding in the center of the purée and top with a flower.

VARIATION:

For variety, substitute sweet white rice for the black sticky rice.

Each serving contains approximately:
140 calories, 1 g fat, negligible cholesterol, 25 mg sodium

EASY ELEGANCE

PAILLARD OF CHICKEN

SERVES 4

Salad of Young Greens
With Signature Dressing

Paillard of Chicken
on Herbed Vegetable Medley

Cherry Berry Clafoutis (see page 96)

Chardonnay or Pinot Noir

One of the easiest yet most dramatic presentations I know for chicken breast is this paillard served on a bed of herbed, lightly steamed vegetables. Everything about this menu is as easy on the cook as it is elegant, beautiful, and healthy!

SALAD OF YOUNG GREENS WITH SIGNATURE DRESSING

MAKES 4 SERVINGS

SIGNATURE DRESSING:

½ cup red wine vinegar

¼ teaspoon freshly ground black pepper

½ teaspoon salt

1 tablespoon sugar

2 garlic cloves, minced

2 tablespoons Worcestershire sauce

2 tablespoons freshly squeezed lemon juice

1 cup water

4 cups assorted young greens, washed and dried (Belgian endive, romaine, radicchio, spinach, watercress, Bibb lettuce, arugula, etc.)

¼ cup Signature Dressing

The dressing for this salad is one I developed for menus at the restaurant at Neiman-Marcus in Newport Beach, California, all of the Four Seasons hotels, and the Canyon Ranch Fitness Resorts. It's also the dressing I keep at home in my own refrigerator.

1. Combine all dressing ingredients and mix well. Refrigerate in a container with a tight-fitting lid. It will keep for months.

2. Arrange greens on 4 chilled plates or in a serving bowl.

3. To serve, spoon 1 tablespoon dressing over each plate or pour ¼ cup dressing over greens in serving bowl and toss.

TIP:

Wash the greens thoroughly to ensure that no grit or sand makes its way into the salad. Also, be sure the greens are dry before you add the dressing; wet greens dilute the flavor of even the tastiest dressing.

VARIATIONS:

Change the flavor of this basic dressing by substituting different herbs and vinegars for those given. You can also add 1 tablespoon oil per cup of dressing, which adds only about 8 calories per serving. Try using raspberry vinegar with walnut oil, or for an Italian dressing add 1 tablespoon olive oil and 1 teaspoon each crushed dried tarragon, oregano, and basil. For a creamy dressing, add to the basic dressing plain nonfat yogurt, low-fat cottage cheese, or tofu and blend until smooth.

Each serving contains approximately:
15 calories, no fat, no cholesterol, 92 mg sodium

NOTE: Nutritional values will vary depending upon the ingredients added to create variations.

PAILLARD OF CHICKEN

The French word "paillard" refers to a fillet of fish, poultry, or meat that has been pounded thin and grilled or sautéed.

1. Place each chicken breast half in a small zip-top bag (which won't stick to the chicken like waxed paper will). Pound each piece to a thickness of ¼ inch with the back of a large spoon or the flat side of a meat tenderizer. Rub each piece with lemon juice.

2. Combine flour, pepper, salt, thyme, sage, and rosemary on a dinner plate. Pour egg whites on another plate. Put bread crumbs in a wide soup bowl.

3. Heat about 2 teaspoons of the oil in a large nonstick skillet over medium-high heat. Dredge chicken breasts in seasoned flour and dust off excess. Dip in egg whites and, finally, in bread crumbs.

4. Cook coated chicken breasts in skillet, about 3 minutes per side or until the chicken turns white and is firm to the touch. Add more oil, as needed. Be careful not to overcook the chicken or it will be dry and tough.

5. Serve atop Herbed Vegetable Medley.

Each serving contains approximately:
336 calories, 6 g fat, 70 mg cholesterol, 679 mg sodium

4 chicken breast halves, boned, skinned, all visible fat removed
Juice of one large lemon
½ cup whole wheat flour
1 teaspoon freshly crushed black pepper
½ teaspoon salt
1 teaspoon dried thyme, crushed
1 teaspoon dried sage, crushed
¼ teaspoon fresh or dried rosemary, crushed
3 egg whites, lightly beaten
2 cups whole wheat bread crumbs
2 tablespoons chopped parsley
1 tablespoon extra virgin olive oil, divided use
Herbed Vegetable Medley (see page 106)

HERBED VEGETABLE MEDLEY

1 medium onion, diced

1 garlic clove, finely chopped

¼ teaspoon salt

1½ teaspoons dried basil, crushed

½ cup chopped parsley

3 cups diced steamed vegetables
   (a colorful assortment)

Vary the vegetables according to whatever is in season.

1. Combine onions and garlic in a pan and cook, covered, over low heat until soft, stirring frequently to prevent scorching.

2. Add salt, basil, and parsley. Mix well and cook 5 more minutes.

3. Add vegetables, mix well, and cook just until thoroughly heated.

NOTE: Nutritional values will vary depending upon vegetables used.

BASTILLA

CROWN JEWEL OF MOROCCAN CUISINE

SERVES 8

Bastilla

*Moroccan Roasted Pepper
and Tomato Salad*

*Basket of Fresh and
Dried Fruits and Nuts*

Mint Tea

B*stila, pastilla, and bisteeya are
some other names for the sweet
and spicy main-dish pastry that
is the centerpiece of this feast
from Fez. It makes a fine party
dish, not only because of its fes-
tive presentation, but because it
can be made ahead, frozen, and
baked without thawing. The salad
and other elements of the meal
also are North African specialties.*

BASTILLA

½ cup raw almonds

½ cup powdered sugar

1 tablespoon ground cinnamon

2 pounds boneless, skinless chicken breasts and thighs

½ teaspoon salt

¼ teaspoon freshly ground black pepper

¼ teaspoon turmeric

½ teaspoon ground ginger

½ teaspoon saffron

⅔ cup boiling water

1 medium onion, finely chopped

1 cup finely chopped parsley

½ cup finely chopped cilantro

2 eggs

4 egg whites

10 sheets phyllo dough

Powdered sugar, for garnish

Ground cinnamon, for garnish

TIP:

Toasting nuts enhances their flavor so much that for most recipes you need only a small amount for a nutty taste. Remember to watch them closely as they toast; the fat in nuts causes them to burn easily.

In Fez this dish is traditionally made with pigeon, for which several of my Moroccan friends find game hens a good substitute. After cooking, skinning, and deboning game hens, however, I decided that chicken breasts and thighs are equally delicious in this dish and infinitely easier to work with!

1. Preheat oven to 350° F. Toast almonds 8 to 10 minutes, or until golden brown. Watch carefully to prevent burning. (Leave oven on for Step 6.) Allow to cool to room temperature and grind coarsely in a blender or food processor. Combine almonds with ¼ cup of the powdered sugar and 2 teaspoons of the ground cinnamon. Mix well and set aside.

2. Place chicken pieces in a Dutch oven or heavy pot and add salt, pepper, turmeric, and ginger. To the boiling water add saffron and stir until dissolved, then add to chicken. Add onion and cook, covered, over medium-low heat until chicken can easily be pierced with a fork, about 30 minutes. Remove chicken from cooking liquid and, using two forks to pull chicken apart, shred it and set aside.

3. Add parsley and cilantro to the cooking liquid in the pot and cook, stirring frequently, until almost dry. In a bowl combine egg, egg whites, remaining ¼ cup powdered sugar, and remaining teaspoon of ground cinnamon. Whip until frothy. Add egg mixture to the pot and cook, scrambling with a fork until almost dry. Stir in shredded chicken and set aside.

4. Spray a heavy, ovenproof 10- to 12-inch skillet with nonstick vegetable coating. Place a sheet of phyllo dough in the skillet, allowing the edges to hang over the sides. Spray phyllo lightly with nonstick coating. Repeat with 3 more sheets of phyllo, spraying each layer.

5. Spread almond mixture evenly over phyllo dough, then top with two sheets of phyllo that have been sprayed and folded in half. Cover this layer with chicken and egg mixture. Fold the overhanging edges of the phyllo over the top of the mixture and again spray the dough. Cover the bastilla with 4 more sheets of phyllo dough, spraying each layer. Neatly tuck the edges of the top layers under the bastilla as you would tuck in bed sheets.

6. Bake at 350° F until golden brown on top, about 20 minutes. Allow to cool slightly and then loosen the bottom of the bastilla with a spatula and slide it out of the pan onto a serving platter. Sprinkle powdered sugar over the top for garnish, and make a criss-cross lattice pattern on the top with ground cinnamon.

Each serving contains approximately:
350 calories, 10 g fat, 126 mg cholesterol, 360 mg sodium

MOROCCAN ROASTED PEPPER AND TOMATO SALAD

MAKES EIGHT ½-CUP SERVINGS

Traditionally made with brine-soaked lemon rind, this salad is more appealing to my taste when made with freshly grated lemon rind.

1. Preheat oven to 475° F. Place pepper quarters, cut side down, on a baking sheet sprayed with nonstick vegetable coating. Bake 20 to 30 minutes, or until skin starts to bubble and turn black.

2. Remove from oven and put immediately in a heavy plastic bag. Seal and allow peppers to sweat for 15 minutes. Remove peppers from bag and slip off and discard the skins.

3. Dice skinned peppers, then combine with remaining ingredients and mix well. Cover and refrigerate until cold before serving.

Each serving contains approximately:
40 calories, 3 g fat, no cholesterol, 155 mg sodium

6 large green bell peppers, seeds and membranes removed, quartered

3 large tomatoes, peeled, seeded, and diced (3 cups) (see page 110)

½ teaspoon salt

1 teaspoon ground cumin
  Cayenne, to taste

1 teaspoon freshly grated lemon rind

4 teaspoons freshly squeezed lemon juice

4 teaspoons extra virgin olive oil

1 cup finely chopped parsley

PEELING, SEEDING, AND CHOPPING TOMATOES

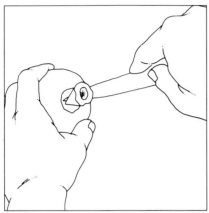

1. Use a paring knife to core the tomatoes.

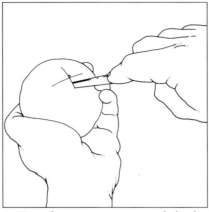

2. Turn the tomatoes over and slit the skin in an X-shaped cut.

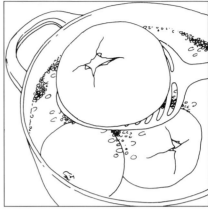

3. Put the tomatoes in a pan containing enough boiling water to cover them and boil for 15 seconds. Remove them with a slotted spoon and put them in a bowl of cold water. Leave for a few seconds.

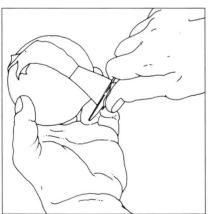

4. Remove them from the cold water and use a paring knife to pull off the skins.

5. Halve the tomatoes horizontally with a chopping knife. Hold each half over a bowl, cut side down, and squeeze to remove the seeds.

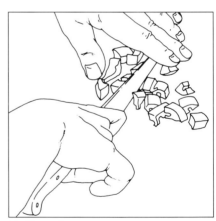

6. Chop the tomatoes.

NON-TRADITIONAL HOLIDAY MENU

SERVES 8

Turkey Lasagne With Cranberries

Pumpkin Pudding

Romano Beans With
Dilled Lemon-Mustard Sauce

Mincemeat "Quenelles"
With Cognac "Crème Anglaise"

Cooked Eggnog and Mineral Water

Serve this unique make-ahead
menu as a holiday dinner or as a
post-holiday meal to use up leftover turkey. The pumpkin pudding makes a pleasant change
from the traditional candied
yams. And just when you thought
a mincemeat dessert was too rich
and high in calories, here's a recipe
that is both tastier and lighter than
you've ever had before.

Turkey Lasagne With Cranberries

Makes eight 3- by 4-inch servings

1½ cups defatted Chicken Stock
  (see page 88)

1 can (12 oz) evaporated
  nonfat milk

2 tablespoons corn oil margarine

3 tablespoons unbleached
  all-purpose flour

¼ teaspoon salt (omit if using
  salted stock)

¼ teaspoon freshly ground
  black pepper

¾ teaspoon dried sage, crushed

1½ teaspoons dried thyme, crushed

3 cups cooked chopped or
  ground turkey

½ cup finely chopped parsley

1 can (16 oz) whole-berry
  cranberry sauce

½ pound lasagne noodles, cooked
  al dente

1 carton (15 oz) fat-free or
  low-fat ricotta cheese

8 ounces shredded part-skim
  mozzarella cheese

¾ cup fresh whole wheat bread
  crumbs (1 slice of bread,
  crumbled)

This holiday-seasoned lasagne is sure to win rave reviews from your family and friends.

1. Preheat oven to 350° F. Combine stock and milk and bring to the boiling point, either in a microwave or on the stove. Melt margarine in a 2- or 3-quart saucepan over medium-low heat. Add flour and cook, stirring constantly, for 2 minutes. Add hot stock and milk mixture, all at once, stirring constantly with a wire whisk. Bring to a boil, reduce heat to low, and simmer, stirring frequently, until liquid starts to thicken, about 5 minutes. Remove from heat and mix in salt, pepper, sage, and thyme. Stir in turkey and parsley and set aside.

2. Spray a 9- by 13-inch baking dish with nonstick vegetable spray. Spread half of the cranberry sauce evenly over the bottom of the dish. Cover sauce with a layer of the cooked lasagne noodles. Top noodles with ricotta cheese and one third of the turkey mixture. Add a second layer of noodles. Spread remaining cranberry sauce over noodles. Cover cranberries with half of the remaining turkey mixture. Sprinkle half of the shredded mozzarella cheese evenly over the top. Cover with remaining noodles, turkey mixture, and shredded cheese. Sprinkle bread crumbs evenly over the top. Bake, uncovered, 30 minutes, or until bubbling and lightly browned. Allow to stand 5 minutes before cutting.

Make-Ahead Tip:

Although everything in this menu can be made ahead, the turkey lasagne is especially flavorful when prepared a day or so in advance. Prepare the recipe up to the point of baking it, then cover and refrigerate. About an hour or so before you're ready to serve the meal, remove the lasagne from the refrigerator and allow it to warm to room temperature while you're preheating the oven. Then bake as directed.

Variation:

If you're cooking for someone with a wheat allergy, omit the bread-crumb topping and substitute 3 cups cooked rice for the lasagne noodles. Simply spread 1 cup cooked rice in place of each layer of noodles.

Each serving contains approximately:
535 calories, 18 g fat, 69 mg cholesterol, 425 mg sodium

PUMPKIN PUDDING

MAKES 3 CUPS, TWENTY-FOUR 2-TABLESPOON SERVINGS

This spice-scented pudding makes a fine sauce for the turkey lasagne. Save any leftovers to spread on sandwiches.

1. Preheat oven to 350° F. Combine pumpkin, cinnamon, nutmeg, vanilla, oil, and honey in a large bowl and mix thoroughly. Add scalded milk and egg whites and again mix well.

2. Pour mixture into a 7- by 11-inch or 8- by 8-inch baking dish and bake for 35 minutes, or until a knife inserted in the center comes out clean. Remove from oven and cool on a rack. Cover and refrigerate until cold before serving.

1 can (16 oz) pumpkin
1½ teaspoons ground cinnamon
¼ teaspoon freshly ground nutmeg
1 teaspoon vanilla extract
1 tablespoon canola oil
¼ cup honey
1 cup nonfat milk, scalded
4 egg whites, lightly beaten

Each serving contains approximately:
29 calories, 1 g fat, negligible cholesterol, 15 mg sodium

ROMANO BEANS WITH DILLED LEMON-MUSTARD SAUCE

MAKES 8 SERVINGS

Serve this easy-to-make recipe either as a first course at the table or as an hors d'oeuvre. If you plan it as an hors d'oeuvre, present the Romano beans unsauced and serve the sauce separately for dipping.

1. Prepare sauce and set aside.

2. Arrange 8 plates with 6 Romano beans on each. Spoon 2 table-spoons Dilled Lemon-Mustard Sauce over each serving, garnishing with a sprig of fresh dill.

Dilled Lemon-Mustard Sauce (see page 58)
48 fresh whole Romano beans, steamed until crisp-tender and chilled
8 sprigs fresh dill, for garnish

Each serving contains approximately:
68 calories, 3 g fat, no cholesterol, 271 mg sodium

Mincemeat "Quenelles" With Cognac "Crème Anglaise"

MAKES EIGHT 6-TABLESPOON SERVINGS

SAUCE:

2 cups melted vanilla ice milk

2 tablespoons cognac or brandy

QUENELLES:

1 box (9 oz) mincemeat (I like Nonesuch brand)

1 pint nonfat ricotta cheese

2 teaspoons vanilla extract

2 tablespoons dark rum, or to taste

These mincemeat dessert dumplings are much lighter and healthier than old-fashioned mincemeat pie, and infinitely easier to make. They taste best when made a day in advance. The sauce, a speedy spinoff of a classic continental custard sauce, saves many grams of fat and hundreds of milligrams of cholesterol.

1. To make sauce, mix melted ice milk with cognac. Set aside.

2. Combine all quenelle ingredients in a food processor fitted with the metal blade and process to a smooth, creamy consistency. Be patient because this takes quite a while.

3. Store, covered, in the refrigerator several hours or (even better) overnight. To serve, form the mixture into three 2 tablespoon–size quenelles for each of the 8 bowls.

3. Spoon 2 tablespoons sauce over each serving.

Each serving contains approximately:
285 calories, 6 g fat, 18 mg cholesterol, 343 mg sodium

COOKED EGGNOG

The best (and safest) eggnog I've ever tasted is one I developed for the California Egg Commission. The commission asked me to revise popular recipes traditionally made with raw eggs by substituting cooked eggs to avoid the possible danger of contamination with salmonella bacteria. If you enjoy eggnog, you'll love the sensational custardy flavor of this version.

4 large egg whites
2 large eggs
1 quart nonfat milk
¼ cup powdered sugar
1 teaspoon vanilla extract
Freshly grated nutmeg, for garnish

1. In a small bowl, lightly beat egg whites and eggs together. Combine milk, eggs, and sugar in a heavy saucepan and mix well with a wire whisk. Slowly bring to a simmer over low heat and simmer 5 minutes, stirring frequently with the whisk.

2. Remove from heat, add vanilla and mix well. Refrigerate until cold.

3. To serve, pour mixture into a blender and add 1 cup crushed ice. Blend until frothy. Pour into cups and garnish with nutmeg.

Each serving contains approximately:
67 calories, 1 g fat, 45 mg cholesterol, 84 mg sodium

MENUS WITH MEAT

Shish Kabob – A Balkan Barbecue

Green Eggs and Ham – A Salute to Dr. Seuss

Greek Family Fare

Fast Food for Kids of All Ages

Company Lamb Chops

MENUS WITH MEAT

Lean meats are completely acceptable in a well-balanced, low-fat diet just as long as they are not served every day and the portions are not too large. Shish Kabob (page 120), Classic and California-Style Burgers (pages 132–133), and Lamb Chops Dijon (page 139) are delicious examples of light, healthy meat entrées you can enjoy with a good conscience. In fact, you can successfully substitute lean meat in many of the recipes in this book calling for fish or poultry, or add it to some of the meatless recipes.

SHISH KABOB

A BALKAN BARBECUE

SERVES 6

Shish Kabob

Light Baba Ghanoush

Cucumber-Yogurt Salad

Whole Grain Rolls

Fresh Fruit

Lemonade, Turkish Coffee,
or Mint Tea

Probably the best known of all
Turkish dishes in the West is shish
kabob. According to legend, it was
a battlefield invention of the Ot-
toman armies. Regardless of its
origins, this spicy skewered meat
is a winner for backyard and
beach barbecues. My favorite accompaniments are minted yogurt
with cucumbers and a baked eggplant purée.

SHISH KABOB

MAKES 6 SERVINGS

MARINADE:

1 medium onion, finely chopped
    (1½ cups)

3 cloves garlic, minced or pressed

1 tablespoon paprika

2 teaspoons ground cumin

1½ teaspoons dried thyme, crushed

½ teaspoon red-pepper flakes

¼ teaspoon salt

¼ teaspoon freshly ground
    black pepper

¼ cup chopped fresh mint

¼ cup chopped parsley

1 tablespoon extra virgin olive oil

KABOBS:

2 pounds boneless leg of lamb
    with all visible fat removed

9 plum tomatoes, halved

1 large red onion, cubed

6 red bell peppers, seeds and
    membranes removed, cut in
    2-inch pieces

12 jalapeño peppers, seeds and
    membranes removed, halved
    (optional)

TIMESAVER TIP:

Many supermarkets now carry cubed lamb for barbecuing. If you can't find it in the meat section, ask the butcher to cut up a leg of lamb for you.

Be sure to put the marinated lamb and each of the vegetables on separate skewers. Tomatoes cook so quickly that they become mushy when grilled the same amount of time as the onions and peppers. Also, putting the meat on separate skewers enables you to grill it to different degrees of doneness to suit individual preferences.

1. Combine all marinade ingredients and mix thoroughly.

2. Cut lamb into 1½-inch cubes, add to marinade, and stir well. Cover and refrigerate several hours or overnight. Remove from refrigerator 2 hours before cooking.

3. Preheat grill or broiler or prepare barbecue for cooking. Remove meat from marinade and put on skewers. Place tomatoes, onions, and peppers on separate skewers to allow for individual cooking times. Place kabobs on a grill over glowing coals or under a broiler, turning occasionally to cook evenly. The lamb cooks in 5 minutes (it is best when served pink). The tomatoes cook in only 1 to 2 minutes; onions and peppers take 3 to 5 minutes.

TIP:
Unless a recipe calls for marinating meat or fish only briefly (for less than half an hour) always marinate these foods in the refrigerator to avoid possible spoilage.

Each serving contains approximately:
340 calories, 13 g fat, 132 mg cholesterol, 202 mg sodium

LIGHT BABA GHANOUSH
(EGGPLANT SIDE DISH, SALAD, OR DIP)

MAKES SIX ⅓-CUP SERVINGS

I have omitted the tahini (sesame seed paste) usually used in this dish to lower the percentage of calories from fat. Instead of the classic garnish of pomegranate seeds, which are often difficult to find, I have added a sprinkling of parsley and mint.

1. Preheat oven to 350° F. Pierce eggplants in several places with the tines of a fork. Place on a baking sheet and bake for 1 hour, then allow to cool.

2. When cool enough to handle, peel eggplants and cut into quarters. Remove all seeds and place eggplant in a colander. Press out liquid and put drained eggplant pieces in a food processor. Add lemon juice, garlic, salt and pepper, and process to a purée. With machine still running, slowly add oil; process until all ingredients are thoroughly combined.

3. Serve immediately or cover and refrigerate. If made ahead, allow eggplant to come to room temperature before serving. Lightly sprinkle with mint and parsley.

TIP:
After the eggplant has baked, be sure to remove the seeds, especially if they are large. If they are left in, the dish may have a bitter taste, and the consistency will not be as creamy as when it is seeded.

2 eggplants (1 lb each)
2 teaspoons freshly squeezed lemon juice
2 garlic cloves, pressed or minced
¼ teaspoon salt
¼ teaspoon freshly ground black pepper
2 tablespoons extra virgin olive oil
Finely chopped fresh mint
Finely chopped parsley

Each serving contains approximately:
70 calories, 5 g fat, no cholesterol, 103 mg sodium

CUCUMBER-YOGURT SALAD

1 large cucumber (14 oz), peeled and cut in half lengthwise

½ teaspoon salt

2 cups nonfat plain yogurt

2 or 3 garlic cloves, to taste, pressed or minced

2 tablespoons extra virgin olive oil

2 tablespoons fresh mint, finely chopped

TIP:

Cucumbers are gourds of the same family as pumpkin and squash. Greenhouse varieties include the 12- to 15-inch English cucumber; outdoor varieties are usually about 8 inches long and 1½ inches wide, tapering at the ends. Choose firm cucumbers that are free of soft spots or puffiness.

This salad is excellent used as a sauce with the lamb.

1. Remove seeds from cucumber by dragging a teaspoon down the center of each half. Grate cucumber and place in a colander. Sprinkle with the salt, then put colander in the sink or over a plate and allow the cucumber to stand and drain for half an hour.

2. Combine yogurt, garlic, olive oil, and mint, and mix thoroughly. Add drained cucumber and again mix well.

Each serving contains approximately:
93 calories, 5 g fat, negligible cholesterol, 258 mg sodium

GREEN EGGS AND HAM

A SALUTE TO DR. SEUSS

SERVES 6

Broiled Grapefruit

Green Eggs and Ham en Croustade

Bloody Mary, Bloody Shame,
or Sparkling Fruit Punch

The late Theodor Geisel ("Dr. Seuss") was one of my favorite authors and also one of my closest friends. He once told me that since publishing Green Eggs and Ham, he'd been served more eggs tinted with green food coloring than he cared to remember. I created this naturally colored, whimsically elegant dish in his honor. The menu is perfect for a sophisticated adult brunch or a child's birthday party.

BROILED GRAPEFRUIT

3 grapefruit
6 fresh raspberries, for garnish
(optional)

Surprise your guests with this healthy, delicious variation on a classic breakfast fruit. Broiling grapefruit brings out all its natural sweetness, so you don't need to add sugar.

1. Cut off a wide piece of the top and bottom of the grapefruit, exposing the inner pith; reserve the ends. Cut grapefruit in half horizontally, then hollow out each half, forming two rings of peel. Place a reserved end inside each ring, cut side up, and press down, creating a bottom for each "bowl."

2. Dice peeled fruit and spoon into grapefruit bowls. Set bowls on a baking sheet and place under the broiler until lightly browned.

3. Top each broiled grapefruit with a raspberry and serve.

Each serving contains approximately:
44 calories, negligible fat, no cholesterol, no sodium

HOW TO PREPARE GRAPEFRUIT

1. Slice off both ends of the grapefruit. Cut the grapefruit in half down the middle.

2. Cut and remove the grapefruit segment, leaving a ring of peel.

3. Fit the cut end and ring together to form a "bowl."

4. Dice the segments and spoon into the grapefruit bowl.

GREEN EGGS AND HAM EN CROUSTADE

MAKES SIX ¾-CUP SERVINGS

If you want to eliminate the cholesterol from the whole eggs in this recipe, I have provided the option of using a liquid egg substitute. Also, the nutritional information assumes that only the lid of the croustade "bowl" is being eaten.

1. Preheat oven to 325° F. To make croustade, slice top off loaf of bread. Carefully hollow out loaf, leaving walls ¾ inch thick. (Save bread crumbs to use in other recipes.)

2. Using a pastry brush, evenly apply 2 tablespoons of the olive oil to entire inner surface of croustade and inside of lid. Bake croustade "bowl" and lid, cut side up, about 25 to 30 minutes, or until well toasted. Remove to serving platter and keep warm.

3. While croustade is toasting, beat egg whites in a large mixing bowl until they form soft peaks; set aside. In a blender, combine milk, chopped parsley, rosemary, thyme, salt, and pepper. Cover and blend until smooth. Turn off blender and add eggs or egg substitute. Cover and blend well. Pour into bowl with egg whites and fold in whites until no streaks of white show.

4. Heat remaining tablespoon of olive oil in large nonstick skillet over medium-high heat. Add garlic and cook just until it sizzles. Add Parmesan and egg mixture, then reduce heat to medium and stir eggs constantly until they are almost set. Add chopped ham and cook until eggs are the desired consistency. Be careful not to overcook eggs—it makes them too dry.

5. Remove eggs from heat and spoon into the warm toasted croustade. Sprinkle chopped parsley over eggs and decorate the platter with sprigs of parsley.

Each serving (with eggs) contains approximately:
369 calories, 21 g fat, 309 mg cholesterol, 1170 mg sodium

Each serving (with egg substitute) contains approximately:
349 calories, 17 g fat, 26 mg cholesterol, 1137 mg sodium

1 large round loaf of whole-grain bread, unsliced

3 tablespoons extra virgin olive oil, divided use

8 egg whites

½ cup nonfat milk

½ cup chopped parsley

½ teaspoon fresh or dried rosemary

½ teaspoon dried thyme, crushed

¼ teaspoon salt (or ⅛ teaspoon if using egg substitute)

½ teaspoon freshly ground black pepper

8 whole eggs (or 2 cups liquid egg substitute)

1 garlic clove, pressed or minced

4 ounces freshly grated Parmesan cheese (1 cup)

6 ounces cooked extra-lean ham, chopped

1 tablespoon finely chopped parsley, for garnish
Parsley or fresh rosemary sprigs, for garnish

TIP:
Herbs also work well to add color to dishes such as rice, polenta, and pasta.

BLOODY MARY (WITH VODKA) OR
BLOODY SHAME (WITHOUT VODKA)

1 teaspoon freshly squeezed
  lime juice
½ teaspoon Worcestershire sauce
¼ teaspoon seasoned salt
  Dash freshly ground pepper
1 cup V-8 or tomato juice
  Dash Tabasco sauce (optional)
1 jigger (3 tablespoons) vodka
  (optional)
2 celery sticks, for garnish

For anyone preferring a savory non-alcoholic brunch beverage, rather than something sweet, this Bloody Shame is the perfect choice. Adding a jigger of vodka increases the calorie count by about 60 calories per serving.

1. Mix lime juice, Worcestershire sauce, seasoned salt, and pepper until salt is dissolved.

2. Add V-8 or tomato juice and mix. Add Tabasco sauce and vodka, if desired.

3. Pour over ice and garnish with a celery stick for a stirrer.

Each serving (with vodka) contains approximately:
76 calories, no fat, no cholesterol, 968 mg sodium

Each serving (without vodka) contains approximately:
28 calories, no fat, no cholesterol, 968 mg sodium

GREEK FAMILY FARE

SERVES 8

Greek Salad With Kalamata Olives
and Feta Cheese

Pastitsio

Baklava

Fresh Fruit

Ouzo or White Wine

This hearty menu features all
time Greek favorites. The salad
is simple but exquisite, relying
for flavor on vine-ripened tomatoes, fresh greens, and a few
Kalamata olives. The main-dish
pasta casserole is ideal for buffet
service because you can make it
ahead and serve it either hot or
at room temperature. This
lighter version of baklava makes
the perfect ending.

GREEK SALAD WITH KALAMATA OLIVES AND FETA CHEESE

MAKES 8 SERVINGS

DRESSING:

½ cup freshly squeezed
  lemon juice

3 tablespoons extra virgin
  olive oil

  Freshly ground black pepper,
  to taste

SALAD:

1 large head romaine lettuce,
  torn in bite-size pieces

8 plum tomatoes, quartered

1 large green bell pepper, seeds
  and membranes removed, cut
  into strips

24 Kalamata olives

1 large red onion, cut into rings

4 ounces feta cheese, crumbled

Imported olives and feta cheese lend a mildly salty flavor to this salad, which perfectly balances the tartness of the lemon juice and the sweetness of the ripe tomatoes. You won't need to add salt, which will also keep your salad greens from wilting if you wish to dress the salad ahead of time.

1. In a small bowl, mix lemon juice, oil, and black pepper and set aside.

2. Arrange 1 cup of the lettuce on each of 8 plates. Add 4 tomato quarters, slices of bell pepper, 3 olives, onion rings, and ½ ounce of the cheese to each salad. Top each serving lightly with lemon juice and oil mixture.

MAKE-AHEAD TIP:

Prepare the dressing and the salads ahead of time and store them, covered, in the refrigerator until you're ready to serve them. Remove the dressing from the refrigerator about half an hour before serving to allow it to reach room temperature.

Each serving contains approximately:
175 calories, 10 g fat, 12 mg cholesterol, 785 mg sodium

PASTITSIO

MAKES EIGHT 1½-CUP SERVINGS

This dish is expandable for large parties. Be sure to use the best-quality Romano cheese you can find for the topping.

1. Cook pasta according to package directions and drain well. Set aside.

2. To make meat mixture, in a large covered saucepan over low heat, cook the onion until soft, about 10 minutes. Stir occasionally and add a little water, if necessary, to prevent scorching. Add lamb and cook until done, about 5 minutes, stirring frequently to keep crumbly. Add tomatoes, tomato sauce, and seasoning; mix well, cover, and simmer 10 minutes, stirring occasionally. Add bread crumbs and mix well.

3. Meanwhile, make the white sauce. Melt margarine in a skillet over medium heat. Add flour and cook 3 minutes, stirring constantly. Add milk, stirring constantly until smooth. Add salt, cinnamon, and white pepper and cook, stirring frequently, until thickened, about 15 minutes. Remove from heat and slowly add egg whites, stirring constantly. Combine 1 cup white sauce with ricotta cheese. Mix well and set aside.

4. Preheat oven to 350° F. Spray a 3-quart baking dish with nonstick vegetable coating. Spread half the cooked pasta in the dish and top with the white sauce without the added ricotta cheese. Spread meat mixture evenly over the top, then sprinkle half the grated Romano cheese over it. Cover with remaining pasta and bake 30 minutes.

5. Remove from oven and increase temperature to 400° F. Spread reserved white sauce over top and sprinkle evenly with remaining Romano cheese. Bake another 20 to 30 minutes, until slightly browned. Cool 10 minutes before serving.

VARIATIONS:
For some interesting variations on the traditional lamb filling for pastitsio, substitute ground chicken, turkey, or beef. For a vegetarian version with an interesting meat-like texture, use crumbled tempeh in place of meat.

Each serving contains approximately:
483 calories, 13 g fat, 61 mg cholesterol, 760 mg sodium

1 package (16 oz) tube pasta

MEAT MIXTURE:
1 large onion, chopped (2 cups)
1 pound lean ground lamb
1 can (16 oz) whole tomatoes, drained and mashed
1 can (8 oz) tomato sauce
½ teaspoon salt
½ teaspoon oregano, crushed
¼ teaspoon ground cinnamon
⅛ teaspoon freshly ground black pepper
1 slice whole wheat bread, toasted and crumbled (¾ cup)

WHITE SAUCE:
3 tablespoons corn oil margarine
⅓ cup whole wheat flour
2½ cups nonfat milk, simmering
½ teaspoon salt
¼ teaspoon ground cinnamon
⅛ teaspoon white pepper
3 egg whites, lightly beaten
½ cup low-fat ricotta cheese

1 cup grated Romano cheese (4 ounces)

BAKLAVA

½ cup walnuts
¼ cup corn oil margarine
¼ cup honey
1 teaspoon ground cinnamon
   Dash of ground cloves
½ teaspoon vanilla extract
6 sheets phyllo dough
¼ cup honey

TIP:

Working with phyllo dough is relatively easy if you handle the dough exactly as the package directions instruct. Place the unopened package of frozen phyllo in the refrigerator to thaw overnight. Remove it from the refrigerator several hours before proceeding with the recipe to allow dough to reach room temperature.

A spa version of a classic dessert for Greek or Middle Eastern menus, this is a recipe I developed for the Canyon Ranch Fitness Resorts. Keep in mind that phyllo, which you'll find in the store's freezer section, has less than half the calories of traditional butter pastry!

1. Preheat oven to 250° F. Using a food processor fitted with the metal blade, grind walnuts to the consistency of coarse meal and set aside.

2. In a saucepan over low heat, combine margarine and honey until margarine is completely melted. Add cinnamon, cloves, and vanilla and mix thoroughly.

3. Spray a 10- by 14-inch baking sheet with nonstick vegetable spray. Place a layer of phyllo dough on a large piece of waxed paper. Using a pastry brush, lightly brush the entire surface with the honey mixture. Add another layer of phyllo and repeat. Sprinkle the second layer with 1½ tablespoons walnuts, leaving a bare edge of dough along one end.

4. Using the waxed paper to help roll the phyllo, roll up (as you would a jelly roll) toward bare edge and close neatly. Place roll on the baking sheet. Brush it with another light layer of honey mixture and slice diagonally into eight even portions, allowing for two half slices at ends. Repeat procedure two more times.

5. Bake about 40 minutes, or until golden brown. Watch closely after 30 minutes; rolls will brown suddenly. Cool on a rack.

6. When cool, warm ¼ cup honey and "paint" the honey on each roll with pastry brush.

Each piece contains approximately:
246 calories, 10 g fat, no cholesterol, 150 mg sodium

FAST FOOD FOR KIDS OF ALL AGES

SERVES 4

*Classic Burger With
Light Hamburger Spread*

*California-Style Burger With
Cranberry Catsup*

Baked Onion Rings

Oven "Fries"

Banana Split

*Flavored Sparkling Water or
Calorie Counter's Wine*

Whatever your age, whatever
your style, you'll find plenty to
like in this new rendition of fast
food. To fit today's healthier, lean-
er nutritional profile, I've updated
everybody's favorite—a burger
with rings 'n' strings—and pre-
sented the burger in classic and
West Coast versions.

CLASSIC BURGER WITH LIGHT HAMBURGER SPREAD

MAKES 4 SERVINGS

LIGHT HAMBURGER SPREAD:

½ cup nonfat mayonnaise

¼ cup bottled chili sauce

2 tablespoons sweet pickle relish

2 tablespoons red wine vinegar

Pinch sugar

Pinch salt

Pinch black pepper

Freshly squeezed lemon juice, to taste

1 pound ground extra-lean beef

4 small whole wheat hamburger buns, split

8 lettuce leaves

8 thin slices tomato

8 paper-thin slices sweet onion

Everybody loves hamburgers. In fact, when I designed this healthier version of the all-American sandwich for the Canyon Ranch Fitness Resorts, it became the most popular item on the menu.

1. Combine Light Hamburger Spread ingredients in a medium bowl and mix thoroughly.

2. Store covered in refrigerator.

3. Preheat grill or broiler. Form beef into four patties and grill until done to taste.

4. Spread 1 tablespoon Light Hamburger Spread on each bun half.

5. Place cooked patties on buns and garnish each serving with 2 lettuce leaves, 2 tomato slices, and 2 onion slices.

Each serving contains approximately:
432 calories, 18 g fat, 98 mg cholesterol, 372 mg sodium

CALIFORNIA-STYLE BURGER WITH CRANBERRY CATSUP

MAKES 4 SERVINGS

This color-keyed hot pink West Coast variation on the traditional burger plate offers unusual eye appeal and sophisticated flavor. You'll never even miss the calories and fat in the original version. Cranberry Catsup is the perfect condiment for a turkey burger and complements any kind of poultry. Try it instead of mayo on post-holiday turkey sandwiches.

1. Pour the water into a small saucepan and add cranberries and onions. Cook over low heat until tender, stirring frequently to prevent scorching. Place in a food processor fitted with the metal blade and process until smooth.

2. Pour the mixture back in the saucepan and add remaining ingredients. Cook until thick, approximately 10 minutes, stirring frequently. Cool to room temperature before serving.

3. Preheat grill or broiler. Form turkey into four patties and grill until done to taste.

4. Spread 1 tablespoon Cranberry Catsup on each bun half.

5. Place cooked patties on buns and garnish each serving with 1 radicchio leaf and 2 onion slices.

Each serving contains approximately:
95 calories, 1 g fat, 1 mg cholesterol, 490 mg sodium

CRANBERRY CATSUP:

¼ cup water

½ pound raw cranberries

½ cup chopped onion

¼ cup frozen unsweetened apple juice concentrate, undiluted

¼ cup white vinegar

⅛ teaspoon ground cloves

½ teaspoon ground cinnamon

½ teaspoon ground allspice

½ teaspoon salt

⅛ teaspoon white pepper

1 pound ground lean turkey

4 small whole wheat hamburger buns, split

4 leaves radicchio

8 paper-thin slices red onion

BAKED ONION RINGS

MAKES 4 SERVINGS

½ cup whole wheat flour
¼ teaspoon salt
1 large onion, cut horizontally and separated into rings
1 egg white, lightly beaten

You don't need a deep fryer and a quart of oil to produce great onion rings. These "oven-fried" rings taste sensational, are easy to make, and won't splatter your kitchen with grease.

1. Preheat oven to 400° F. Cover a baking sheet with parchment paper or spray with nonstick vegetable coating. Combine flour and salt in a paper bag and shake to mix well. Set aside.

2. Steam onion rings over rapidly boiling water for 3 minutes. Rinse with cold water to stop the cooking; drain well.

3. In large bowl combine onion rings with egg white and mix well. Put onion rings one at a time into bag with flour and salt and shake to coat thoroughly. Remove from bag and place on the baking sheet, being careful that rings do not overlap.

4. Spray onion rings liberally with nonstick vegetable coating and bake 15 minutes. Turn rings over with a fork or tongs, spray again with nonstick coating, and bake 10 more minutes. Serve immediately.

Each serving contains approximately:
35 calories, negligible fat, no cholesterol, 81 mg sodium

OVEN "FRIES"

MAKES 4 SERVINGS

2 unpeeled baking potatoes

Who says fries have no place in light cuisine? Besides being a snap to make, these "fries" taste like real potatoes, not grease!

1. Preheat oven to 375° F. Spray a baking sheet heavily with nonstick vegetable coating.

2. Scrub potatoes and slice into french fry strips slightly thicker than shoestring potatoes. Arrange potato strips on baking sheet so that they do not touch. Spray lightly with nonstick vegetable coating.

3. Bake 1 hour. Serve hot.

Each serving contains approximately:
65 calories, 1 g fat, negligible cholesterol, 12 mg sodium

BANANA SPLIT

MAKES 4 SERVINGS

A *fun dessert to serve anytime, and you needn't feel guilty for indulging. If you don't have soda-fountain dishes for serving up the splits, use individual gratin dishes.*

1. Preheat oven to 350° F. Toast almonds until golden brown, 8 to 10 minutes. Watch carefully; they burn easily. (Nuts can also be toasted in a toaster oven or dry skillet.) Set aside.

2. Place 2 scoops of ice milk in each of 4 banana-split dishes. Slice each banana in half lengthwise. Place a banana half on each side of dish.

3. In each dish, pour ¼ cup Chocolate Sauce over one of the scoops of ice milk. Pour ¼ cup Strawberry Topping over remaining scoops.

4. Sprinkle 1 teaspoon toasted almonds over each banana split. Place a strawberry half on top of each scoop of ice milk, if desired.

Each serving contains approximately:
195 calories, 4 g fat, 5 mg cholesterol, 63 mg sodium

12 raw almonds, chopped
2 cups vanilla ice milk
4 small bananas
1 cup Chocolate Sauce (recipe follows)
1 cup Strawberry Topping (recipe follows)
4 large, perfect strawberries, halved (optional)

CHOCOLATE SAUCE:

Much *lower in saturated fat than most bottled chocolate sauces, this one is made with cocoa powder instead of bar chocolate.*

1. In a saucepan over medium heat, scald milk. Meanwhile, in another saucepan over medium heat, melt margarine. Add cocoa to melted margarine, mix thoroughly, and cook for about 3 minutes. Do not brown.

2. Remove cocoa mixture from heat and add scalded milk all at once, rapidly whipping with a wire whisk. Add sugar and return mixture to medium heat and simmer, stirring with whisk, until sauce reaches desired thickness.

Each serving (¼ cup) contains approximately:
220 calories, 5 g fat, 1 mg cholesterol, 119 mg sodium

CHOCOLATE SAUCE:

1 cup nonfat milk
1½ tablespoons corn oil margarine
⅓ cup unsweetened cocoa powder
⅔ cup sugar

STRAWBERRY TOPPING:

2 cups fresh or frozen
  unsweetened strawberries

1 teaspoon freshly squeezed
  lemon juice

⅓ cup sugar

½ cup water

1 tablespoon arrowroot powder

TIMESAVER TIP:

To make a banana split in almost
no time at all, use low-calorie bottled chocolate sauce and a jar of
all-fruit strawberry jam, and leave
out the toasted almonds.

STRAWBERRY TOPPING:

*I always make more of this recipe than I need for the banana splits.
That way I'm sure to have some left over to spread on French toast,
pancakes or waffles the next morning. I also like this topping on hot
cereal with a little yogurt on the side.*

1. In a heavy saucepan over very low heat, cook berries, covered, for
   about 10 minutes. Uncover, bring to a boil, and boil for 1 minute.
   Remove from heat, add lemon juice and sugar, and mix well.

2. In separate pan, combine the water and arrowroot and bring to a
   boil. Simmer until mixture is clear and slightly thickened, about 2
   minutes. Remove from heat and allow mixture to cool to room
   temperature.

3. Add arrowroot mixture to berries and blend well. Allow topping
   to cool to room temperature and store in the refrigerator.

Each serving (¼ cup) contains approximately:
47 calories, negligible fat, no cholesterol, 1 mg sodium

CALORIE-COUNTER'S WINE

Dry red, white, or rosé wine

*Removing the alcohol in wine means fewer calories. This recipe
calls for boiling the wine, so pick an inexpensive bottle and save
your most valuable vintage for another occasion.*

1. Pour wine into a nonreactive saucepan and slowly bring to a boil.

2. When wine starts to boil, hold a lighted match with long kitchen
   tongs (at least 8 inches long) and ignite the wine. Allow it to burn
   until flames go out, indicating that most of the alcohol has been
   consumed. The volume of wine will be reduced by the volume of
   its alcohol content.

3. Allow wine to cool to room temperature, then store tightly covered in the refrigerator. Serve red wine at room temperature and
   white or rosé wine chilled.

Each 3-ounce serving contains approximately:
60 calories, negligible fat, no cholesterol, 2 mg sodium

COMPANY LAMB CHOPS

SERVES 8

Sherried Pea Soup

Lamb Chops Dijon

Rosemary Bread Sticks

Herbed Brussels Sprouts
and Tomatoes

Virtuous Cheesecake

Merlot or Pinot Noir

This menu is ideal for busy people who like to entertain. You can prepare the lamb chops many hours in advance or even the day before. In fact, every dish in this menu can be made ahead to free you for enjoying time with your family and guests. An added plus is that everything but the lamb can be served cold or at room temperature.

SHERRIED PEA SOUP

MAKES EIGHT 1-CUP SERVINGS

4 cups Chicken Stock (see page 88)

6 cups green peas, fresh or frozen

½ teaspoon white pepper

¼ teaspoon salt (omit if using salted stock)

2 teaspoons sugar

2 cups nonfat milk

⅔ cup sherry

TIP:

My rule of thumb for cooking with wine and sherry is to never cook with anything you wouldn't drink. So-called "cooking wine" and "cooking sherry" have salt added, a custom that dates from the times when the wine to be used in the king's kitchen was salted to discourage the cooks from drinking it up. Today these products can be sold in stores without liquor licenses. Poor-quality alcohol taints the flavor of any dish, so always cook with table-quality wine or sherry.

Although you can serve this soup hot or cold, for this menu I like to serve it chilled, as the first course.

1. Combine in a pan all ingredients except milk and sherry and bring to a boil.

2. Reduce heat, cover, and simmer 3 to 5 minutes or until peas are tender.

3. Pour mixture into a blender. Add milk and sherry and blend until smooth. To serve cold, pour into chilled bowls or cups.

Each serving contains approximately:
76 calories, negligible fat, 1 mg cholesterol, 176 mg sodium

LAMB CHOPS DIJON

MAKES 8 SERVINGS

I like lamb chops crusty on the outside and bright pink and juicy on the inside, which is just the way they'll turn out using this cooking method. If you prefer lamb chops well done, bake them for 5 minutes instead of 4 before turning off the oven.

1. Preheat oven to 500° F. Remove all visible fat from lamb chops and place them in a flat baking dish. Rub both sides of each chop with lemon, then sprinkle with garlic salt and pepper.

2. Combine mustard, bran, and parsley and mix well. Cover each lamb chop with some of the parsley mixture, pressing it down firmly with your hands.

3. Bake 4 minutes, then turn oven off and do not open the door for 30 minutes. If you leave the chops in a little longer they will not overcook.

MAKE-AHEAD TIP:
You can prepare the lamb chops many hours in advance or even the day before you serve them. Simply prepare them up to the point of baking, cover them tightly, and refrigerate until you are about 30 minutes away from serving the meal. Then bake the chops as directed and serve.

Each serving contains approximately:
248 calories, 11 g fat, 91 mg cholesterol, 612 mg sodium

8 lamb chops, 1½ inches thick
2 lemons
  Garlic salt
  Freshly ground black pepper
⅔ cup Dijon-style mustard
2 tablespoons unprocessed wheat bran
2 cups finely chopped parsley

TIP:
This method of roasting lamb chops also works well with other kinds of chops, steaks, and small roasts. And the best part is that after the first 4 (or 5) minutes of cooking the meat doesn't require watching. You can simply set the timer and go about other kitchen tasks. When the timer rings, the meat's done to a turn.

ROSEMARY BREAD STICKS

1⅓ cups low-fat milk, warmed

4 teaspoons baking powder

1¼ teaspoon salt

1½ teaspoons finely chopped fresh
  rosemary, crushed

¾ teaspoon cracked black pepper

½ cup minced green onions

1⅓ cups whole wheat flour

1⅓ cups unbleached all-
  purpose flour

Besides being delicious and low in fat, these bread sticks are easy to make and a delight for the eyes. Try other herb and spice variations, such as thyme or cumin, in place of the rosemary.

1. Combine warm milk, baking powder, salt, rosemary, pepper, and green onions in a large bowl and mix well. Stir in flour and turn onto a floured board. Knead dough until it becomes smooth and elastic, about 5 minutes, adding a little more flour if necessary. Allow to rest for 30 minutes at room temperature.

2. Preheat oven to 375° F. Divide dough into 16 equal balls, about 1¼ ounces each. Roll each ball into a long, thin rope. Place them on a baking sheet sprayed with nonstick vegetable spray. Lightly spray bread sticks with nonstick spray and bake about 12 minutes, or until bottoms are golden brown. Turn bread sticks over and bake until the other side is brown, about 10 more minutes.

Each bread stick contains approximately:
84 calories, 1 g fat, 1 mg cholesterol, 295 mg sodium

HERBED BRUSSELS SPROUTS AND TOMATOES

4 cups (1 lb) Brussels sprouts

2 tablespoons olive oil

¼ teaspoon salt

1 tablespoon finely chopped
  fresh basil or 2 teaspoons
  dried, crushed

¼ cup finely chopped parsley

¼ cup finely chopped green onions

4 cups (1½ lbs) cherry tomatoes,
  stems removed

If you thought you didn't like Brussels sprouts, try this recipe. A member of the cabbage family, Brussels sprouts are native to northern Europe. Paired with cherry tomatoes, they make an attractive, tasty side dish that's delicious hot or cold.

1. Steam Brussels sprouts only until crisp-tender, about 8 to 10 minutes.

2. In a large frying pan heat olive oil until fragrant. Add salt, basil, parsley, and onions and sauté over low heat, until onions are translucent.

3. Add Brussels sprouts and tomatoes and cook, tossing gently, until heated through, about 2 to 3 minutes.

Each serving contains approximately:
65 calories, 3 g fat, no cholesterol, 89 mg sodium

VIRTUOUS CHEESECAKE

MAKES 8 SERVINGS

The first time I tasted this practically fat-free cheesecake I didn't believe it was as virtuous as I was told. Much to my surprise, the recipe is as healthy as it is delicious.

1. Preheat oven to 325° F. Spray a 9-inch pie plate with nonstick vegetable coating. Add crumbs and shake plate to coat entire surface. Set aside.

2. Combine cream cheese, sugar, and flour in a large mixing bowl. Beat with electric mixer on medium speed until thoroughly mixed and creamy. Beat in sour cream, egg whites, and vanilla. Pour mixture into prepared crust and place in center of oven. Bake 40 minutes, remove from oven and cool on a rack. Refrigerate 3 hours before serving.

3. Cracks will form in the top of the cheesecake during baking and cooling. If you wish to cover these cracks before serving, spoon sliced strawberries over cheesecake.

VARIATION:
For an easy and unusual holiday dessert, use one 16-ounce can of whole-berry cranberry sauce in place of the strawberries.

½ cup graham cracker crumbs
2 cartons (8 oz each) nonfat cream cheese
½ cup sugar
1 tablespoon unbleached all-purpose flour
½ cup nonfat sour cream
3 egg whites
1 teaspoon vanilla extract
2 cups sliced strawberries (optional)

Each serving contains approximately:
170 calories, 1 g fat, 12 mg cholesterol, 115 mg sodium

U.S. Measure and Metric Measure Conversion Chart

Formulas for Exact Measures

Measure	Symbol	When You Know	Multiply By	To Find
Mass (weight)	oz	ounces	28.35	grams
	lb	pounds	0.45	kilograms
	g	grams	0.035	ounces
	kg	kilograms	2.2	pounds
Volume	tsp	teaspoons	4.9	milliliters
	tbsp	tablespoons	15.0	milliliters
	fl oz	fluid ounces	29.57	milliliters
	c	cups	0.237	liters
	pt	pints	0.47	liters
	qt	quarts	0.95	liters
	gal	gallons	3.785	liters
	ml	milliliters	0.034	fluid ounces
Temperature	° F	Fahrenheit	5/9 (after subtracting 32)	Celsius
	° C	Celsius	9/5 (then add 32)	Fahrenheit

Rounded Measures for Quick Reference

Mass (weight)	1 oz	=		30 g
	4 oz	=		115 g
	8 oz	=		225 g
	16 oz	=	1 lb	= 450 g
	32 oz	=	2 lb	= 900 g
	36 oz	=	2¼ lb	= 1000 g (1 kg)
Volume	¼ tsp	=	1/24 oz	= 1 ml
	½ tsp	=	1/12 oz	= 2 ml
	1 tsp	=	1/6 oz	= 5 ml
	1 tbsp	=	½ oz	= 15 ml
	1 c	=	8 oz	= 250 ml
	2 c (1 pt)	=	16 oz	= 500 ml
	4 c (1 qt)	=	32 oz	= 1 liter
	4 qt (1 gal)	=	128 oz	= 3¾ liter
Temperature	32° F	=	0° C	
	68° F	=	20° C	
	212° F	=	100° C	

Equivalents

Beverages

Coffee	
Beans, ground	*1 pound, 80 tablespoons = 40 to 50 cups brewed*
Instant	*4-ounce jar = 60 cups brewed*
Ice cubes	*2 = ¼ cup melted*
Tea leaves	*1 ounce = 20 cups brewed*

Cereals and Grain Products

Bread crumbs	
Soft	*1 slice = ¾ cup*
Dry	*2 slices = ½ cup crumbled; 4 slices = ½ cup finely ground*
Bulgur	*⅓ cup = 1 cup cooked*
Cornmeal	*1 cup = 4 cups cooked*
Flour	
All-purpose	*1 pound = 4 cups*
Cake	*1 pound = 4½ cups sifted*
Whole wheat	*1 pound = 4 cups*
Graham crackers	*14 squares = 1 cup finely crumbled*
Oatmeal, quick-cooking	*1 cup = 2 cups cooked*
Rice	
Brown	*1 pound, 2½ cups = 7½ cups cooked*
White	*1 pound, 2½ cups = 5 cups cooked*
Wild	*5⅓ ounces, 1 cup = 3½ to 4 cups cooked*
Soda crackers	*21 squares = 1 cup finely crumbled*

Cheese

American	*¼ pound = 1 cup grated*
Blue	*5 ounces = 1 cup crumbled*
Cheddar	*¼ pound = 1 cup grated*
Cottage cheese, not packed	
Large curd	*8 ounces = 1 cup*
Small curd	*7½ ounces = 1 cup*
Dry curd	*5½ ounces = 1 cup*
Cream cheese	*3-ounce package = 6 tablespoons*
Monterey jack	*¼ pound = 1 cup grated*
Parmesan	*3½ ounces = 1 cup grated; 3 ounces = 1 cup shredded*
Ricotta, whole or part-skim	*8½ ounces = 1 cup*
Swiss	*¼ pound = 1 cup grated*

Eggs

Raw	
Whole	*6 medium = 1 cup*
Whites	*1 medium = 1½ tablespoons; 8 medium = 1 cup*
Yolks	*1 medium = 1 tablespoon; 16 medium = 1 cup*
Hard-cooked	*1 medium = ⅓ cup finely chopped*
Egg substitute, liquid	*¼ cup = 1 egg*

Fish and Shellfish

Anchovy	*3 fillets, drained and chopped = 1 teaspoon*
Crab	*½ pound, fresh, frozen, cooked, or canned = 1 cup*
Lobster	*½ pound, fresh or frozen, cooked = 1 cup*
Oysters	*½ pound, raw = 1 cup*
Scallops	*½ pound, fresh or frozen = 1 cup*
Shrimp	*1 pound, shelled and cooked = 3 cups*
Tuna	*6- to 7½-ounce can, drained = ¾ cup*

Fruits (Dried)

Apples	*1 pound = 8 cups diced*
Apricots	*1 pound = 8 cups diced*
Dates	*1 pound whole, 2½ cups = 1¾ cups pitted and chopped*
Figs	*1 pound, 2½ cups = 4½ cups cooked; 2 cups chopped*
Pears	*1 pound, 3 cups = 5½ cups cooked*
Prunes, pitted	*1 pound, 2½ cups = 3¾ cups cooked*
Raisins, seedless	*1 pound, 2¾ cups = 3¾ cups cooked; 2 cups chopped*

Fruits (Fresh)

Apples	*1½ pounds, 6 small = 4 cups sliced; 4½ cups chopped*
Apricots	*1 pound, 6 to 8 average = 2 cups chopped*
Avocado	*1 medium = 2 cups chopped*
Bananas	*1 pound, 4 small = 2 cups mashed*
Blueberries	*1 pint = 2 cups*
Cherries	*1 pound, 2 cups = 1 cup pitted*
Cranberries	*1 pound = 4½ cups whole; 4 cups chopped*
Figs	*1 pound, 6 to 8 small = 2 cups chopped*
Grapefruit	*1 small = 1 cup sections*
Grapes	
Concord	*¼ pound, 30 grapes = 1 cup*
Thompson seedless	*¼ pound, 40 grapes = 1 cup*
Guavas	*1 pound, 4 medium = 1 cup*
Kumquats	*1 pound, 8 to 10 average = 2 cups sliced*
Lemon	*¼ pound, 1 medium = 3 tablespoons juice; 2 teaspoons grated zest*
Limes	*½ pound, 5 average = 4 tablespoons juice; 4 to 5 teaspoons grated zest*
Loquats	*1 pound, 5 average = 1½ cups chopped*
Lychees	*1 pound, 6 average = ½ cup chopped*
Mangoes	*1 pound, 2 average = 1½ cups chopped*
Melon	
Cantaloupe	*2 pounds, 1 average = 3 cups diced*
Crenshaw	*3 pounds, 1 average = 4½ cups diced*
Honeydew	*2 pounds, 1 average = 3 cups diced*
Watermelon	*10 to 12 pounds, 1 average = 20 to 24 cups cubed*
Nectarines	*1 pound, 3 average = 2 cups chopped*
Oranges	*1 pound, 3 average = 1 cup juice, 3 cups sections*
Papaya	*1 pound = 2 cups cubed, 1 cup puréed*
Peaches	*1 pound, 3 average = 2 cups chopped*
Pears	*1 pound, 3 average = 2 cups chopped*
Persimmons	*1 pound, 3 average = 2 cups mashed*
Pineapple	*3 pounds, 1 medium = 2½ cups chopped*
Plums	*1 pound, 4 average = 2 cups chopped*
Pomegranate	*¼ pound, 1 average = 3 cups seeds*
Prunes	*1 pound, 5 average = 2 cups chopped*
Raspberries	*4½ ounces = 1 cup*
Rhubarb	*1 pound, 4 stalks = 2 cups chopped and cooked*
Strawberries	*5 ounces = 1 cup*
Tangerines	*1 pound, 4 average = 2 cups sections*

Herbs, Spices, Seasonings, and Gelatin

Garlic powder	*¼ teaspoon = 2 small cloves fresh garlic*
Gelatin, powdered	*1 envelope = 1 scant tablespoon*
Ginger, powdered	*½ teaspoon = 1 teaspoon grated fresh ginger*
Herbs, dried	*½ teaspoon crushed = 1 tablespoon fresh*
Horseradish, bottled	*2 tablespoons = 1 tablespoon fresh*

Legumes

Chick-peas	*1 pound, 2 cups = 6 cups cooked*
Kidney beans	*1 pound, 1½ cups = 4 cups cooked*
Lentils	*1 cup = 2 cups cooked*
Lima	*1 pound, 2½ cups = 6 cups cooked*
Navy beans	*1 pound, 2½ cups = 6 cups cooked*
Split peas	*1 pound, 2 cups = 5 cups cooked*

Meat and Poultry

Bacon	*1 slice, cooked = 1 tablespoon crumbled*
Chicken	*3½ pounds, roasted, boned, and skinned = 3 cups chopped*
Escargots	*6 = 1½ ounces*
Meat	*1 pound, raw, cubed or chopped = 2 cups tightly packed*

Milk and Milk Products (Except Cheese)

Butter and margarine	*¼ pound, 1 cube = ½ cup (8 tablespoons)*
Cream, whipping	*1 cup = 2 cups whipped*
Powdered milk	
Buttermilk, powdered	*3 tablespoons + 1 cup water = 1 cup buttermilk*
Instant nonfat	*⅓ cup + ⅔ cup water = 1 cup nonfat milk*
Noninstant nonfat	*3 tablespoons + 1 cup water = 1 cup nonfat milk*
Whole	*¼ cup + 1 cup water = 1 cup whole milk*
Nonfat, canned	*1 cup = 5 cups whipped*

Nuts

Almonds	*32 whole = ¼ cup chopped; 8 whole = 1 tablespoon chopped*
Brazil nuts	*½ pound = 1½ cups*
Coconut	*½ pound shredded = 2½ cups*
Macadamia	*3 whole = 1 tablespoon finely chopped*
Peanuts	*44 whole = ¼ cup chopped; 11 whole = 1 tablespoon chopped*
Pecans	*20 halves = ¼ cup chopped; 5 halves = 1 tablespoon chopped*
Walnuts	*12 halves = ¼ cup chopped; 3 halves = 1 tablespoon chopped*

Pasta (Dried)

Linguine noodles	*1 pound = 5 cups cooked*
Macaroni	*1 pound, 5 cups = 12 cups cooked*
Asian noodles	*¾ pound = 5 cups cooked*
Rotelle pasta	*1 pound, 4 cups = 6 cups cooked*
Rotini pasta	*½ pound, 3 cups = 4 cups cooked*
Spaghetti	*1 pound = 8 cups cooked*

Vegetables (Fresh)

Artichokes	*½ pound = 1 average*
Arugula	*½ pound = 2 cups bite-sized pieces*
Asparagus	*1 pound, 18 spears = 2 cups 1-inch pieces*
Beans, green	*1 pound = 5 cups 1-inch pieces*
Beets	*1 pound, 5 average = 6 cups sliced; 2½ cups cooked*
Bell pepper	*½ pound, 1 large = 1 cup seeded and finely chopped, 2 cups sliced*
Broccoli	*1 pound, 2 stalks = 6 cups chopped and cooked*
Brussels sprouts	*1 pound, 28 average = 4 cups*
Cabbage	*1 pound = 4 cups shredded; 2½ cups cooked*
Carrots	*1 pound, 6 medium = 4 cups grated; 3 cups sliced*
Cauliflower	*1½ pounds, 1 average head = 6 cups chopped and cooked*
Celery	*½ pound = 1½ cups chopped; 1 stalk = ½ cup finely chopped*
Celery root	*1¾ pounds, 1 average = 4 cups grated; 2 cups cooked and mashed*
Chiles, jalapeño	*¼ pound, 8 chiles = 1 cup chopped*
Corn	*6 ears = 2½ cups cut, whole kernels; 2 cups scraped flesh and liquid*
Cucumber	*½ pound, 1 medium = 1½ cups sliced; 1 cup diced*
Eggplant	*1 pound, 1 medium = twelve ¼-inch slices; 6 cups cubed*
Garlic	*1 clove = 1 teaspoon finely chopped*
Leeks	*1 pound = ½ pound, white part only; 2 cups chopped; 1 cup cooked*
Lettuce	*1½ pounds, 1 average head = 6 cups bite-sized pieces*
Mushrooms	*½ pound = 2 cups sliced*
Onions	
Yellow	*½ pound, 1 medium = 1½ cups finely chopped*
Pearl	*10 ounces = 2 cups*
Green	*4-ounce bunch, 6 average = 1 cup chopped*
Parsley	*1 pound = 8 cups tightly packed, 8 cups finely chopped; 2 ounces = 1 cup tightly packed, 1 cup finely chopped*

Parsnips	1 pound, 6 average = 4 cups chopped
Potatoes	1 pound, 2 medium = 3 cups coarsely chopped; 2½ cups cooked and diced
Pumpkin	3 pounds, 1 average = 4 cups cooked and mashed
Radicchio	10 ounces, 1 average head = 2½ cups bite-sized pieces
Rutabagas	1½ pounds, 3 small = 2 cups cooked and mashed
Shallots	¼ pound = ¼ cup chopped
Spinach	1 pound = 4 cups bite-sized pieces; 1½ cups cooked
Squash	
Acorn	1½ pounds, 1 average = 2 cups cooked and mashed
Banana	3 pounds, 1 average = 4 cups cooked and mashed
Chayote	½ pound, 1 average = ½ cup diced; ¾ cup sliced
Spaghetti	5 pounds, 1 medium = 8 cups cooked
Summer	1 pound, 4 average = 1 cup cooked
Zucchini	1 pound, 2 average = 3 cups diced; 4 cups thinly sliced; 1½ cups cooked and chopped
Tomatillos	¼ pound, 4 small = 1 cup chopped
Tomatoes	1 pound, 3 medium = 2 cups peeled, seeded, and chopped; 1¼ cups cooked and chopped
Turnips	1 pound = 2 cups peeled and grated; 4 cups bite-sized pieces; 1¼ cups cooked and mashed
Watercress	¼ pound, 1 bunch = 1 cup loosely packed

EQUIPPING THE '90s-STYLE KITCHEN

For Measuring

Measuring cups (1-cup liquid measure; 2-cup liquid measure; set of dry measure cups ranging from ¼ to 1 cup)

Measuring spoons (¼, ½, and 1 teaspoon; ½ and 1 tablespoon)

Kitchen scale

Utensils and Gadgets

Grater (one with fine holes; one with large holes)

Knives (French, paring, serrated, and sharpening steel)

Mortar and pestle

Pepper mill

Rolling pin

Spoons (metal and wooden; slotted and solid)

Spatulas (wide and narrow; rubber and metal)

Timer (stand-alone or built into the stove)

Tongs

Wire whisk

For Mixing, Steaming, Straining

Colander

Mixing bowls (ceramic or stainless steel)

Steamer basket

Strainer (metal)

Electric Appliances

Blender or food processor

Electric mixer

For Cooking and Baking

Baking pans (8- by 8-inch square, 9- by 5-inch rectangle, 9- by 5-inch loaf pan, 9-inch round cake pan, rimless cookie sheet, 10- by 15-inch rimmed jelly-roll pan, muffin pan)

Nonstick sauté pans (8-, 10-, 12-inch, with lids)

Saucepans or pots (1-, 2-, and 3-quart)

Large pot with lid

Dutch oven

Wire rack

For Storage

Plastic wrap

Aluminum foil

Parchment paper

STOCKING THE '90S-STYLE PANTRY

Fresh Herbs (If fresh herbs are not available, use dried and crush in a mortar and pestle before using.)
Basil
Bay leaves
Dill
Marjoram
Oregano
Rosemary
Sage
Tarragon
Thyme

Spices
Allspice
Cayenne
Chili powder
Cinnamon
Cloves
Cumin
Curry
Ginger
Nutmeg
Pepper
Red pepper flakes
Saffron
Salt
Tumeric

Extracts
Almond
Coconut
Rum
Vanilla

Produce
Garlic
Onions
Parsley
Potatoes
Shallots

Dairy Products
Butter or margarine
Eggs
Milk (skim or low-fat)
Parmesan cheese

Oils
Canola or corn oil
Dark sesame oil
Extra virgin olive oil

Vinegar
Balsamic vinegar
Cider vinegar
Red wine vinegar
Rice vinegar
Sherry vinegar

Wine
Marsala
Red wine
White wine

Mustard
Brown
Dijon-style
Dry

Canned and Packaged Goods
Artichoke hearts
Chiles
Clams
Fruit
Roasted red peppers
Sun-dried tomatoes
Tomato paste
Tomato sauce
Tuna

Other
Beans
Brown sugar
Chicken and beef stock (homemade in freezer or canned low-sodium in refrigerator)
Confectioners' sugar
Gelatin
Low-sodium soy sauce
Pasta
Peanut butter
Rice
Sugar
Tabasco/hot sauce
Worcestershire sauce

INDEX

ACKNOWLEDGMENTS

Jeanne Jones would like to thank the following: Betty DeBakcsy; Nancy Ann Chandler; Chef Matthew Kenney of Matthew's in Manhattan; Lorenza d'Medici's Cooking School, Tuscany, Badia a Coltibuono; Patrick McDonnell, Director of Recipe Development for Con Agra for Healthy Choice™; The Ritz Cooking School in Paris; The Thai Cooking School in Bangkok; Anne Willan, La Varenne in Burgundy (Paris Cooking School).

Joyce Oudkerk Pool, Elisabeth Fall, and Barbara Berry would like to thank the following people for all their help, support, kindness and props: Biordi, San Francisco; Echo, San Francisco; Cha Am Thai Restaurant/Bar & Grill, San Francisco; Cafe Tiramisu, San Francisco; Michel D'Amico; Pam Nagle; Evolutions, San Francisco; Dr. Robert Veder; Andronico's Butchers; Monterey Market; Bernadette Lau.